Praise for /

Working with Alan is like

These principles have helped me prepare for the opportunities and challenges of various seasons. The tools help me make healthy, intentional decisions for myself, my family and my company.
—Jenn, Founder and CEO, Denver

During an extremely pivotal time in my life and career Alan helped me answer questions I didn't even know I was asking. He didn't tell me what to do—he coached me with love, understanding, and clarity.
—Chaz, YouTuber, Los Angeles

Alan Briggs has been one of the greatest catalysts in my life for personal and professional progress. So much of the momentum I'm currently experiencing is a result of his tools and insight. This book is an investment with the potential to give you ridiculous returns for your journey.
—Johnny, Business leader, Connector and Author, Colorado Springs

If you're in charge of a team send your folks to something Stay Forth is doing—or better yet, participate with them!
—Angie, Co-founder and COO, Denver

The true gift of Alan's coaching is his ambidexterity, as he toggles between personal and professional contexts. His nimble listening, structured feedback and constructive criticism helped opaque areas of my leadership become crystal clear.
—Wayne, Pastor and NBA Chaplain, New York

Alan's coaching modeled 'working from rest' in a way I had not seen before. He provided empowering guidance and tools to realize the vision I was given.
—Sean, NonProfit Founder, Arizona

Working with Alan helped me to realize that behind a healthy business is a healthy human. His coaching directly impacted the health and progress of our business.
—Seth, Business Owner, Colorado

Alan coached me on the tangible pieces of my business and also coached my soul. I can't say enough about my life improvement after my coaching with Alan.
　　　　　　　　　　—Laura Beth, Business Coach, Nashville

My wife and I launched a business that would still be a mere idea if it wasn't for Alan's coaching.
　　　—Matt, Nonprofit Executive and Business Leader, Detroit

My toxic workaholism nearly killed me. Alan's coaching and tools saved my marriage, put me on a pathway to health and freedom, and restored my soul. There was no fluff, and no B.S.
　　　　　　—Ron, Business and Nonprofit Leader, New Jersey

Without Alan, I honestly don't know where I'd be. Navigating burnout, career changes and family priorities with him revealed his passion for guiding folks through their journey.
　　　　　　　　　—Rhys, Business Owner, New Hampshire

As an accidental entrepreneur, working with Alan completely changed my outlook on how to intentionally build my business. He kept me from giving up and instead helped me to cultivate a business I'm passionate about while growing a team, taking time for rest and pursuing longevity.
　　　　　　　　　　　—Amy, Business Owner, Colorado

I am so grateful for Alan coaching me through complex seasons with grace and confidence. Thanks to him, I'm thriving in my role, have found a healthy balance, and am a better wife, mother, and friend.
　　　　　　　　　　　　—Caitlin, COO, Philadelphia

I discovered Alan prior to a massive professional and personal transition. He diagnosed issues within me I wasn't aware of and provided practical steps for my leadership. Alan is a fantastic human and an amazing coach.
　　　　　　　　　　　—John, Business Operator, Texas

The tools, experiences and strategic guidance Alan has given me have been life-giving and at points, life-saving. With his help, I emerged stronger, healthier, and more effective after a painful career transition. When the only way out is through, Alan is the perfect traveling companion, guide, and friend.
—Steve, Leadership Coach, Denver

Alan's writing and coaching have helped me find more effectiveness and fulfillment as a leader. He has helped me realize my leadership gifts and given me tools to better equip me as I equip others.
—Russ, Pastor, Louisiana

I always leave my sessions with Alan less confused and overwhelmed and feeling more optimistic about my trajectory as a leader for the long-haul!
—Kory, Nonprofit founder and CEO, Indiana

Alan has helped me find the courage to explore hidden paths and unnoticed opportunities. I find myself with a renewed energy, a refreshed confidence, and a deeper hope.
—Justin, Coach and Spiritual Director, Colorado

Hardback ISBN number 979-8-9900652-0-8
Paperback ISBN number 979-8-9900652-1-5
All right reserved
Copyright Alan Briggs 2024

AntiBurnout is published by Far Peak Press
No portion of this book may be reproduced without the consent of the author
Cover design and tool design by Daron Short
Layout by Beryl Glass

Want to buy a lot of these books or go deeper? For bulk discounts, speaking or coaching in these principles **hello@stayforth.com**

A lighter way
to live and lead
in a heavy world

Alan Briggs

To all those I've had the privilege of coaching

Thanks for trusting me.

Your hunger and constant growth inspire me.

CONTENTS

PART ONE
Dispatches for the climb

The Safety Talk; warnings before you climb. 15
The Opposition; burnout 21
The Preparation; training for health 31
The Topography; constant change 43
The Route; your pathway up the mountain 49

PART TWO
Obstacles and opportunities along the climb

The Obstacle: Overwhelm—The Opportunity: Clarity. . . . 61
The Obstacle: Stuckness—The Opportunity: Newness. . . . 67
The Obstacle: Exhaustion—The Opportunity: Replenishment . 75
The Obstacle: Change—The Opportunity: Experimentation . . 87
The Obstacle: Pain—The Opportunity: Connection 91
The Obstacle: Disappointment—The Opportunity: Naming . . 99
The Obstacle: Resistance—The Opportunity: Movement . . . 103
The Obstacle: Cynicism—The Opportunity: Curiosity 107

PART THREE
Shifts to lighten the load

From reactive to proactive 115
From confusion to clarity 119
From triage to priorities 123
From time management to energy investment 127
From intuitive to intentional 131
From doer to developer 135
From efficient to effective 139

PART FOUR
Habits to keep you climbing

Learn like your life depends on it (because it does) 147
Seize little slivers of opportunity 153
Don't just feedback, feed-forward 157
Accept that you'll never be "over the hump" 161
Create more than you consume 163

Care more than everyone else 167
View sales as an invitation. 171
Cultivate empowerment, not dependency 175
Work from rest, don't rest from work 179
Optimize your schedule (especially your meetings) 183
Learn to live whelmed 187
Ditch hype, cultivate hope. 191
Create the safety to risk (and fail). 195
View your limits as a gift 199
Remember what got you here won't get you there 201
"Waste" time on a hobby 205
Go slow or go fast, but don't rush 207
Don't forget people are the killer app 211
Build your process. Then trust it. 215
Imitate until you innovate 219
Be accessible, not available 221
Stop adding value; multiply it 227
Stay (constantly) aware of your season 231
Utilize rest and momentum to your advantage 235
Show your work 241

PART FIVE
Essentials for the long climb
Sleep, routine, spiritual connection, exercise, work boundaries, caffeine and adrenaline, diet, technology and
relational connection. 247

PART SIX
Practices for the climb
Recovery, physical health, mental health, emotional health, vocational health and relational health 253

CONCLUSION
The old man and the hourglass 259

Recommended resources to go deeper 260

Before you start reading

Before you climb, launch or lead something it's important to define what you're aiming at. Take a few minutes to set some hopes and expectations before you begin.

What one thing am I hoping for from this book?

Which area of my life or leadership feels heaviest right now?

Which area of my life or leadership needs some lift right now?

If that area got lift what else in my life could change?

If I burned out what would the consequences be?

I have leveraged my life into helping leaders find freedom. I have distilled these principles, tools and ideas directly from thousands of hours coaching leaders just like you. I would love to get an email from you sharing how this book changed the trajectory of your life. It's hard work, but it IS possible to lead well for the long haul without burning out.

Climb on!

Alan Briggs
Alan@StayForth.com

PART ONE
Dispatches for the climb

THE SAFETY TALK
warnings before you climb

Courage and fear are not mutually exclusive.
Most of us feel brave and afraid at the exact same time.
Brené Brown[11]

Being a mountain guide is the the most exhausting job I've ever had. I lived on the side of a mountain at 10,000 feet in rural Colorado. Groups would come from the flatlands to experience a week in the mountains. No hot tubs, ATV excursions or lodges with an elk mounted above a giant fireplace. We did, however, offer port-o-potties, meals packed with carbs, nightly temperatures close to freezing and a chance to toughen up. Groups arrived from the airport struggling to breathe the thin air with heads pounding from an altitude headache.

The apex of the week was a guided climb up a 13,450 foot mountain. We gave each group a customary safety talk at the beginning of the week with the basics of living at altitude, mostly how bears would love to grab your Snickers out of your sleeping bag. One group of high school girls forgot the "don't drink from the streams" part of the talk; we found them lapping water directly from a stream flowing through a cow pasture. That must've been a fun next week.

We gave the real safety talk the night before the peak climb. We warned of the dangers of the mountains, and let them know what to expect. We would also try to scare a few folks away from the climb. Honestly, it was way better to have folks hang back at basecamp than turn around halfway. Through sweat, blisters, dehydration and plenty of tears I had the great joy of standing on top of mountains with people who never thought they could do it. It was exhausting and thrilling.

Climbing mountains humbles you quickly. Weather turns nasty at altitude. I've lost my way in whiteouts, traversed glaciers ready to fall on my ice axe if a fellow climber slid into a giant crevasse, crossed small ledges that would've ended me and turned around a few times when fellow climbers fell sick. I've also stood on top of peaks in tears hugging friends who had become comrades during the climb. In a sea of towering peaks you become refreshingly tiny.

Leading is humbling, too. Last week I got three texts sharing how vital my coaching had been, a painful call telling me I had accidentally devalued someone and the confirmation that we had to delay a project launch. Climbing mountains is no joke. Leading isn't either.

Leading and climbing are harrowing and fulfilling, challenging and rewarding. They have plenty of highs and plenty of lows. The consequences are real, and, at times we wonder, "Is this really worth it?" Leaders look ahead and make the best decisions they can. They read the contours and topography of the land and help teams climb ahead. We can't predict the future, but we do get to shape it.

I labored over these words, because I want you to be fulfilled, healthy and climbing more mountains for many years to come. I'm sick of burnout stories. But just as a mountain guide can't carry a client to the summit no coach, mentor or boss can carry you up your leadership climb. You've got to want it. You've got to keep climbing amidst the fear and pain. Each week I feel the joy, the thrill, the challenge and the victory of helping leaders and teams climb and summit their mountains.

Leading is weighty. Sometimes the exhaustion of making decisions, organizing information and working with teams gets us down. As a Leadership Coach I have a unique vantage into the joys and

PART ONE | Dispatches for the climb

challenges leaders face. I help leaders in various industries navigate twists and turns for the majority of my week. The role is strangely similar to a mountain guide. If you're a leader seeking to steward the influence you have you bear an immense weight. You're doing a really hard thing, and I want to help you lighten the load. A guide cannot climb the peak for a climber, but they can help navigate the route and lighten the load in your pack.

This book will help you lighten the load you're carrying as a leader. Don't worry; this isn't full of cheap tricks— "7 leadership hacks to change your life in the next 15 minutes" or an *"Introduction to Leadership"* course to convince you to lead someday. I won't cheapen the challenge and sacrifice of leading. Leadership is full on, but it's worth it. These words, principles and tools have been forged on the trails and peaks of leading. I'm honored to help incredible leaders across the country and across industries navigate their climbs.

All great adventures come with warnings: whitewater rafting, skydiving, bungee jumping, field trips in elementary school (clearly the best part of school), even marriage. When we see a safety warning it means there's adventure on the other side. After you sign the eighteen page waiver (no, I've never read one fully- have you?) there's a safety talk full of more warnings. Before we embark on this expedition here's your safety talk.

Leading is hard. I'm not one of those guys who says, *"Leading is awesome. Everyone should do it!"* If you've accepted the invitation to influence others, serve, make hard decisions and be an example you're carrying some weight. It's incredibly fulfilling, but it can be tiring and feel unfair and lonely. Some days it will break your heart. It has also gotten increasingly heavy and complex in recent years. My aim is to give you strategies to take some weight off your shoulders and simplify some of the complexity.

This book isn't for everyone. I speak, write, coach and consult toward those who see themselves as people of influence. Perhaps you view yourself as a leader among friends, family or in your community but don't have a formal title. Perhaps others report to you at work, or you lead a large team. I aim squarely at people who know their influence matters. I'm not trying to convince anyone their actions bear weight; I assume you already know that quite well.

There's a lot at stake. I believe every human matters deeply, they can make an impact on those around them and they are capable of huge things. Life is short, and how we carry ourselves will shape others. Leaders can cause destruction and create environments of dignity. When leaders are healthy hundreds or thousands around them benefit.

People can change. At my core I believe people can change. I get to watch this unfold each week, and people around me have been patient with me to invite me to change (you know who you are). Clarity is a stimulant to change (I'll also refer to it as *awareness*) that invites us into courage (I'll also refer to it as action). Once you have taken new steps I will challenge you to create consistent habits in order to actualize change. I look forward to getting your emails sharing the changes you've made and the victories you've experienced.

I aim at being helpful, not exhaustive. I'm not trying to go to the depths of any topic in this book. Everything I'm writing goes through the filter of, *"Is this helpful for a leader carrying weight?"* That's why I often start sections with stories of real leaders I've worked with who overcame real barriers and experienced real change. I'm not pulling this stuff out of thin air. I include some of my favorite books at the end in case you want to dig deeper on one subject.

You won't agree with everything I say. Not only am I okay with that, but that's healthy. Think through these ideas, and test drive them in real life. I respect you enough as a reader and leader to say things bluntly. I'm not beating around the bush and wasting your precious time.

I've practiced these principles in public. As a coach, consultant, podcaster and speaker I've learned from some amazing leaders. These ideas, concepts and phrases were developed or refined through failure, success, group work, cohorts, masterminds and one-on-one coaching sessions. These aren't just ideas I'm trying out; they are practical handles forged from years of coaching conversations. I've watched them bring lightness to others, and I hope they lighten your load.

I am a person of faith. My coaching work is grounded by my faith in God, but I don't write in a language of faith. I believe each person is

PART ONE | Dispatches for the climb

uniquely designed by God and worthy of dignity and respect. I promise not to beat you over the head with anything I believe, but love is the foundation of my work.

I wrote this as a real person to other real people. I'm a dad of four kids, husband to one wife, an active community member and a business owner. I have plenty of responsibilities, friends I care about and hobbies I love. I've been through a lot of hard seasons and thought about quitting more than a few times. There have been moments I thought "the dream" was done, we wouldn't make payroll, or the next project was too daunting. I write to real people, not avatars. I picture a tired mom pulling into the garage after a hard day at work, an intimidated middle manager taking on a daunting project or a terrified young leader staring their goal in the face.

I'm far from perfect, and so are the leaders I write about, but I've experienced a lighter way to live and lead that I didn't know was possible. And I love watching others experience that, too. Jump around this book to the sections you need most. I'm a big fan of expectations, so I wanted to give you these warnings right out of the gates. There's your safety talk. Grab your pack. It's go time.

THE OPPOSITION
burnout

Fatigue makes cowards of us all.
Hall of Fame football coach Vince Lombardi

I was simultaneously coaching two leaders who were experiencing deep pain. They were both in similar roles and felt deep purpose in the professions they had chosen. They both lived near major cities in similar sized homes, had multiple children and were experiencing similar exhaustion in their work. I processed their struggles openly with both of them. They weren't bad leaders; they had a dysfunctional relationship to their work.

After processing the need for serious changes both went to their bosses and explained their challenge and were met with very different reactions. One had a boss who validated burnout was a real danger and allowed him time off to breathe and replenish. During this time he made a proactive decision to make internal and external changes to his rhythms and habits personally and professionally. The other boss did not allow the leader time off and, instead, continued to push harder on this leader for results. He spiraled into depression and serious despair and was diagnosed with occupational burnout. The impact of burnout was devastating for he and his beautiful family.

Both ultimately moved to new states and transitioned to new roles shortly after this challenging season. One had the wind to their back and the other carried loads of pain, resentment and baggage with him. I realize every human is carrying a unique load, and we all respond to situations differently. But I am struck by how two very different responses by two bosses impacted these leaders so profoundly; one heeded the red dashboard lights of burnout, the other continued with business as usual.

The burnout epidemic
We are in the midst of a burnout epidemic. You can find it in every industry, sector and age group. I'm not trying to be negative; only to paint a realistic picture of what we're facing. Burnout is real. Burnout is dangerous. Burnout is widespread. We must be aware of it for ourselves, those we love and those we work with so we can make adjustments.

The bad news; burnout is stealthy. It sneaks up on us.

The good news; when watching for burnout we can take action against it.

After years of watching burnout pop up in conversations in nearly every field and group I worked with I felt compelled to make a shift to focus on health in addition to impact. This book has sprouted directly from that commitment.

In the course of a three year period, I watched leaders who I thought were burning bright make sudden decisions to quit, relocate across the country and take shelter for healing. "What is going on?!" I wondered. As I met with and coached leaders in different fields I saw the same thing. Everywhere. Burnout isn't just coming for founders and entrepreneurs; it's coming for everyone. You either know someone who has burned out or you are that person.

A few years ago I got to lead a group coaching experience with faith and community leaders in Ecuador. On the long flight I wondered, "Will they be able to relate, or is this just another American issue?" We began our gathering by gauging their level of tiredness. Much to my surprise they seemed to wrestle with the expectations to care for families, communities and congregations even more than we do in the

West. Their fatigue levels were high, and they were constantly leaving the room to take calls.

I was speaking through a translator, and she wrestled for the right words to describe burnout. A man came up to the translator and whispered the word "fundido" to her. The translation — *"an engine that seizes up from running hot with no oil."* Nailed it! I couldn't understand most of their discussion and banter, but one discussion got heated. A younger leader called an older leader to the carpet for his statement "We'll rest when we're dead! Our communities need us". The younger leader quipped back, "If you do not rest you will be dead!" Touché.

The Korean language now has its own world for 'working yourself to death' — *"gwarosa."*[2] Alex Pang reports that "Koreans now work more hours per year than almost any other country in the world. Suicide rates have tripled since 1990.

In his book The Burnout Society researcher Byung-Chul Han shares the widespread effects of burnout. He says, "Twenty-first century society is no longer a disciplinary society, but rather an achievement society."[3]… The society of laboring and achievement is not a free society. It generates new constraints. It leads to a society of work in which the master himself has become a laboring slave" [4] "The achievement subject is simultaneously perpetrator and victim, master and slave."[5] It's not just something that is done to us, but many times we allow it, even perpetuate it.

Burnout is particularly common among high achievers. Teachers and University professors have been hit hard. Over fifty percent of medical professionals live close to burnout. Pastors have felt increased expectations over the last decade to care for communities while providing excellent gatherings live-streamed to the world. Entrepreneurs feel the deep weight of risk and failure especially during unsteady markets. Young companies normalize the pressure of their work as they joke about "riding the rocket" of exponential growth (sounds painful). Research seems to show burnout coming particularly hard and stealthy for women, who often bear more relational responsibility in their homes than men.[6] Many parents even report parental burnout from increased expectations to get their kids involved in everything under the sun.[7]

What is burnout?

Before we talk about a lighter way to live and lead we must clearly define what we're actually talking about. The term "burnout" was formally introduced to the world by psychologist Herbert Freudenberger in 1975. He defined burnout as a *"state of mental and physical exhaustion caused by one's professional life."*[8] It had three defining factors.

Emotional exhaustion; the fatigue that comes from caring too much, for too long.
Depersonalization; the depletion of empathy, caring and compassion.
Decreased sense of accomplishment; an unconquerable sense of futility.[9]

Sound familiar? Here are some other clinical definitions of burnout from experts.

"A response to the chronic emotional strain of dealing extensively with other human beings, particularly when they are troubled and having problems"[10]
"A syndrome of emotional exhaustion and cynicism that occurs in individuals who do 'people work' of some kind"[11]
"A chronic state of feeling overworked, overwhelmed and exhausted"[12]
"Voluntary self-exploitation"[13]

That's what the experts say. But how do normal humans describe burnout? I asked a group of friends who have experienced burnout, "What did burnout feel like?"

Emptier than empty
Running at 8,000 RPMs with no true sense of any measurable progress
Freezer burn — loss of quality, flavor and nutrients
Full, yet completely empty
Doubting every move I made
Depleted mentally and emotionally, unable to recharge
Ice skating uphill
Numb
A complete lack of care that I no longer really care

Drowning
The pain of knowing you will never be able to get ahead
Spiritually and emotionally fried to a crisp
Trying to run through quicksand blindfolded
Overwhelm followed by anxiety, depression and guilt
Trying to run through an ocean of molasses

Burnout can be easily misunderstood. Here's what we're not talking about when we describe burnout. Burnout is not just...
Physical tiredness, although that's one symptom
Grief, although unrealized grief can perpetuate it
Inevitable, it doesn't have to be this way!
Sacrifice, although unmeasured, unwise sacrifice can be part of it
Sudden, although it can feel like it
Failure, although it can slow us down
Easy to notice in ourselves, others can see if far easier than we can
The end, although it may feel like it

Dr. Wes Beavis describes the burnout risk zone using the following equation:

$$\textit{dealing with people}$$
$$+$$
$$\textit{being responsible for favorable outcomes}$$
$$=$$
$$\textit{Burnout Risk Zone}[14]$$

This equation puts all leaders in or near the risk zone. Inherently, leaders are responsible not only for their results, but for others results. Seth Godin says, "If you are using outcomes that are out of your control as fuel for your work, it's inevitable that you will burn out. Because it's not fuel you can replenish."[15] The challenge is real for leaders, and none of us is immune. We cannot give what we do not have. Trying to give others what we do not possess ourselves will empty us. Giving what we do not have is not generosity; it's stealing. When we do this we are the perpetrator and the victim.

What are the results of burnout?

Every human is unique and burnout can look different for each person, but here are some common consequences.

Burnout hurts our health and our families. Burnout limits our capacity for empathy and compassion for those around us, and can spiral into depression. It hurts us and those we love the most.

Burnout stunts our decision making. When we're exhausted and overwhelmed we think reactively, not proactively. The tyranny of the urgent rules us and leaves us with drunken decision making.

Burnout slows down our teams and organizations. Burnout decreases our productivity, and often creates abrupt exits from an organization. These transitions slow down our teams and organizations. Replacing these positions costs billions of dollars to the workforce annually.

Burnout caps our compassion and creativity. As we get closer to burnout we lose creative sharpness and potential to innovate. "Compassion fatigue" is a synonym to burnout. Without compassion and creativity we cannot solve the crucial problems in front of us, and problem solving is, of course, a critical part of leadership.

Burnout blinds us. Ironically, we are often the last to see our own exhaustion, overwhelm and burnout. Others around us notice our tiredness, apathy or grumpiness before we do. It not only blinds our vision of ourselves, but it also blinds our vision of the future. It leads to tunnel vision, causing us to think small and immediate instead of large and future-oriented.

Stretching the limits

We've stretched the limits in nearly every area of life, and we're paying the price. Our cultural quest to live limit-less is breaking us down. Let's look at the following areas.

Relational limits. How many people can we have meaningful relationships with? Experts have come to different answers on this. Dunbar's number is around 150, but others say as many as 290. Compare those we follow and follow us on social media, hear us give talks or listen to our podcast. We've stretched our relational limits far beyond what we were designed for.

Physical limits. We hop across the country instantaneously on zoom calls. We "pound through" a stack of emails, drive quickly around town for meetings and hop on a plane for a quick business trip or vacation. We keep our bodies moving faster than we were designed to go doing more tasks than we were designed to do while giving our bodies less nutrients and sleep than they were designed to have.

Mental limits. Our brains feel constantly full from taking in more information than we can process. We're mentally overloaded with information from our inbox to our news feed to our LinkedIn. Decision fatigue plagues many leaders today. Our craniums are getting fuller, but we're not getting wiser.

Emotional limits. Every day we hear about new threats, atrocities and painful losses from our own city to the farthest reaches of the earth. We simply weren't designed to respond to and empathize with all the pain and unrest we see in the world.

Spiritual limits. Many have lost connection with churches and religious groups they grew up in. Work has become a religion of sorts and a place where we seek deep meaning. Our society has become cynical from being let down by spiritual authorities and those in positions of power. Our souls are weary and undernourished.

Financial limits. Our finances are stretched, and we're spending above our limits. This stress to make ends meet drives people to advance their career or launch a side gig in their spare time.

Great news! You can't do it all

Imagine you just finished an incredible dinner with dear friends. The environment was amazing, the food was delightful and the wine was impeccable. You held nothing back; laughs, challenges and encouragement. After four amazing courses they bring out a fine chocolate mousse that blows your mind. Four hours disappear, and you come back to life again after a stressful week. When you give hugs and get into your car you think, "this is the good stuff in life right here." Your belly and heart are full; full of delight, full of joy, full of gratitude.

Experiencing fullness is very different from gorging ourselves. What if your life **was more like a beautiful meal with friends and less like** over-eating at a potluck? How might our lives change if we viewed them as wonderfully full instead of frantically busy? We desperately need to reframe how we see our time and priorities. How we view our lives and our schedules becomes a self-fulfilling prophecy. Telling ourselves we're busy produces more busyness.

> How might our lives change if we viewed them as wonderfully full instead of frantically busy?

Several years ago I quit using the four letter word *busy* and traded it for the other four letter word; *full*. My mindset shifted. I began to see the gift of a full life. I instantly felt grateful for opportunities to invest in my family and my community. I reframed opportunities to connect with friends without cramming them in my schedule. I redesigned my work schedule to serve my clients better while not driving me to exhaustion. My wife and I have a lot of responsibilities with four kids, two full-time jobs and a community we love dearly, but we also take time to get away and create margin through a weekly sabbath. It is possible to live a full life and still have margin.

Busy has become normal. People often start conversations with "I know you're busy but...". Perhaps they are projecting their busyness on us, or they cannot imagine how we braid the aspects of our lives together. Like our stomachs when we really want that key lime pie, our schedules stretch to fit the things we really desire (the "dessert stomach" is a true wonder). But part of what makes life beautiful is savoring the moment. Instead of cramming more into our lives we can be fully present, fully attentive, fully alive.

If you ask your next ten coffee or lunch dates, "How are you?" I bet eight of them will say "busy." It's the marker of our culture, and it's even worse for leaders. We live in a culture stricken by "hurry sickness"[16] Greg McKeown, author of the bestseller *Essentialism*, says, "Our culture glorifies burnout as a measure of success and self-worth. The implicit message is that if we aren't perpetually exhausted, we must not be doing enough. That great things are reserved for those who bleed, for those who almost break."[17] If you believe busyness is inevitable your actions will fulfill that. We cannot reverse the burnout cycle until we go head-to-head with our broken beliefs about our busyness.

Our busyness is a self-created cycle, and it can be a self-broken cycle, too. Most people in our culture are over-filled and under-nourished. If we tell ourselves we're busy we'll stay busy. But if we tell ourselves we have a full life that is full of meaningful things we can savor them. *No* is a magic word. Remember, you can say *no* to good things like parties, networking lunches, travel soccer for your kids, coffee with friends or watching your friend's dog. Healthy people get used to the sting of disappointing others.

Our schedules reveal what we believe about time. Our habits tell on us. If you're weary or feeling stuck in your schedule there's great news; you have limits. You cannot do it all. You can make tough decisions and disappoint people without your world falling apart.

Many times burnout is a result to perpetual overwhelm and a stuck mindset. One of the greatest whispers that normalizes excessive work and overwhelm says, "Leading will always be like this. If you want to lead at a high level you have to work yourself to the bone and make every possible sacrifice."

If you need a phrase to put on a sticky note on your mirror try this one; *I cannot do everything I want to do, but there is enough time to fulfill my priorities.*

If you'll do anything to get impact you'll do ANYTHING to get impact

Abuses of power are eroding our trust. When we hear another scandal break we wonder, "How could that leader ever do that heinous act?" The root of these mistakes can be exhaustion. In this place of exhaustion anyone can sink to levels they had never imagined and make choices they never comprehended. I'm not excusing wrong behavior or abuses of power, we can and must do better! Aiming at professional success at all costs will yield a narrow-mindedness and exhaustion that will wear us down. If our deepest desire is success we will yield to the whispers of success over the shouts of our family, our organization and our health.

Exhaustion is not the only thing that leads people compromise. When we use our work to fight for our worth it ends poorly. Leading in order to prove something to ourselves and others will cause us to use people instead of serving them. This insecurity can leave leaders riding an emotional rollercoaster, feeling untouchable on their best days and worthless on their worst days. If you are so driven that you will do anything, absolutely anything, to get impact then you'll sink to do anything, yes anything, to get impact. You are not the sum of your work.

When leaders are out to prove something they will eventually carry deep weight. We need a lighter way to live and lead, one where we live like humans, not machines. One where we carve a path toward flourishing and joy, not toward exhaustion and continuous overwhelm. Let me go ahead and give you permission to rest, permission to make mistakes, permission to not grind yourself down every week in search of success.

If you find yourself depleted and exhausted right now you need to tell someone. You aren't alone; many have been here before. But you cannot continue drifting. Too much is at stake! Take a rest break and change your pace, but please don't quit climbing the mountain in front of you. I'm glad you picked up this book. I've walked with leaders who make changes to their life and leadership and find a healthy, sustainable groove. Yes, it is possible

Reflect on burnout

What was the unhealthiest time in my life or leadership?

What events or beliefs led me here?

What areas of my life or leadership are unhealthiest right now?

What are some specific steps I can take toward health in these areas?

THE PREPARATION
training for health

Nearly all men can stand adversity,
but if you want to test a man's character, give him power.
Abraham Lincoln

A friend introduced me to a leader he admired who was growing a company. He thought our organizations could partner together to serve more leaders. From my first conversation with Todd I could tell he was driven and innovative with serious business acumen. His team was growing, and he was hiring quickly. We discussed a potential partnership. He promised to get back with me on a few ideas. Not only did he not get back with me, but he ghosted me.

Months later our mutual friend told me he was in our town for meetings, and I should join them for a drink. That evening he apologized for not getting back with me, and I observed him making big promises and bragging about big contracts. He assured me we would reconnect, but he ghosted me again. About eighteen months later I got a desperate text from him requesting an emergency coaching session. His life and business had fallen apart, and he needed help sorting out the wreckage.

We don't need more like Todd's. How many times do we have to watch the same worn out stories; a brilliant leader that people follow wholeheartedly drifts from their integrity, hurts the people they love and leaves a wake of destruction. A great company with great products who employed great people simply couldn't maintain the success, because they became unhealthy. Scandals broke, money was misused, promises weren't kept.

> We desperately need healthy women and men shaping the future who leverage their influence to serve others, not themselves.

This can happen to us if we ignore personal and organizational health. Yes, ANY of us. Somehow health feels too simple, too elementary. Leading can feel weighty. You're already climbing a mountain, and people add baggage to your pack. Sometimes the weight on leaders shoulders feels too much to bear. Leadership is a serious climb that impacts us and many around us. We must fight for a lighter way to live and lead.

Before we push on take a moment to pause reflect.
What feels heavy right now?
The expectations others have of you?
The reality that you're putting your family on the back burner?
The pressure of hitting your goals?
The shame from not hitting last year's goals?
The multiple responsibilities you're juggling in your role?
The gnawing feeling that you're doing too much?

Shaping the future

Leaders shape the future. Martin Luther King Jr. and Hitler both shaped the future in very different ways. We are still in the wake of both of their actions today. We desperately need healthy women and men shaping the future who leverage their influence to serve others, not themselves.

The most challenging changes leaders make aren't "out there", they're "in here." We must look inward first before we look to the horizon. We

PART ONE | Dispatches for the climb

must do the hard internal work of change before we hope to make great changes in the world. Growth has very little to do with the position of the leader and a lot to do with their posture. Look at the unlikely people who have shaped the world; Rosa Parks, Ghandi, Greta Thunberg, Jesus, Brian Stevenson. These revolutionaries began on the fringes and stirred up transformative mischief that changed the world.

Perhaps you're trying to launch a profitable businesses, be a present father, lead a nonprofit shaping your community, unify people amidst a divided culture or reform a cracking system. Whether you're in the position of an entrepreneur, a middle manager, a parent, a CEO, a teacher, a pastor or a solo-preneur you can shape the future. Will the future be better because you shaped it?

In his book *The Advantage* business consultant and thought leader Patrick Lencioni says, "The single greatest advantage any company can achieve is organizational health…it is the single greatest factor determining an organization's success"[18] He points to some markers of health; "minimal politics and confusion, high degrees of morale and productivity and very low turnover among good employees"[19]. Wouldn't all of us who run companies want those things? Wouldn't every employee want to show up to those things every day at work? But none of those happen overnight or accidentally. They take years of intentional decisions. They require a belief that health is worth investing in for years until they run through the bloodstream.

Of course, leaders and teams must be excellent at their craft constantly working to grow and bring their best. I don't minimize leadership competency, but it's simply a baseline to be in our field. Lencioni has observed that healthy teams actually get greater over time as they get healthier[20]. It requires a lot of work, but investing in personal, professional and organizational health is worth it.

All leaders carry some kind of power. Dr. Henry Cloud says, "As a leader, your position carries much more psychological and emotional weight than you know"[21] As leaders we carry a power dynamic. Be careful; when we speak people may treat our words as gospel truth. They may withhold information from us for fear of being fired. People watch (sometimes "stalk") leaders like a hawk from up close and online. It's sobering to think of the impact we have on others. The way leaders carry their power and influence sends a message.

Most leadership training and education focuses on information and competency. Very few every learn how to pursue health and structure for longevity. I love helping gifted leaders cultivate their health so they can continue doing great work for a long time. I want to help leaders discover health and impact, to look back and say, "I'm so glad I invested in the things that matter most to me!". I want to be more in love with my wife, Julie, decades from now. I want my kids to know they were, and are, my priority for their whole lives. I want to take care of myself so I can be effective for a long time. Sustainability requires different thinking and different actions.

When I made the decision to focus my coaching agency, Stay Forth, on the health of the leader first and on the impact to the leader second I thought I was on a kamikaze mission. "No one wants to focus on health; everyone is yearning for more impact", I thought. But leaders kept requesting my help to align with the things that mattered most to them. Then a pandemic exposed our dark side. We brushed up against our limits as the pandemic squeezed our families and organizations. We realized we were a hot mess. That season gutted many organizations and humbled and awakened many leaders, myself included.

Health has never been sexy, but the longer we last the more we realize how vital it is. We've gravely underestimated health. Just talk to anyone over seventy years old living with vitality, and they'll tell you their habits for staying healthy. Leadership is a long climb, a war of attrition that can wear us down slowly. People choose to stop climbing, turn around and head back down the mountain every week. We all must ask ourselves the question, *"Do I have healthy habits in place?"* If not, it's time to develop them.

The 4H Leader

How can we predict who is ready to change? The greatest changes happen internally, and there's no sure bet, but I look for four markers in leaders. I call leaders who posses them "the 4H leader".

Humble. Growth starts with the awareness that you need to grow. This means you don't know everything, and you must learn in order to show up the best you can. This humility will magnetize you to mentors, coaches, leaders and authors who have been where you want to go. Humble leaders walk into every room knowing they have something to learn, and are okay saying, "I don't know".

Hungry. Only the hungry grow. Hungry people find a way to get over their barriers. They're willing to stay longer, work harder than the rest, ask the uncomfortable questions and do the assignments. Hungry leaders will squeeze the most out of this book. I challenge you to slow down and reflect on the questions, fill in the tools and write down the next steps that can change your life.

Healthy. We're tired of selfish leaders with poor integrity. People are crying out for healthy servants and stewards to lead them. Hoards of people have migrated from jobs where they felt like machines treated as mere dollar signs and squeezed for more production at any cost. This is not the way forward for work! It can't be. I'm crazy enough to believe it's possible to live and lead healthy and be excellent at our craft without burning out, flaming out or abusing our power.

Honest. There is nothing more refreshing than a leader who isn't hiding anything. When a client shares where they're stuck, confused or overwhelmed I get excited. When we're honest with ourselves and those around us we set a course for change. People across industries are done with the know-it-all leader, and increasingly drawn to the vulnerable leader. I invite you to be honest with your challenges and struggles as you read through this book.

I hope you smell a fresh scent of optimism throughout this book. I hope you hear the audacious claim that leading can and must be lighter.

The spiritual and the practical

If you've led for longer than a few years you know you'll face hard times. You're going to hit criticism, recessions, doubters and plenty of moments when you're backed into a corner. Lots of folks back out and move on during hard times. If you've continued leading through these you believe it's worth it. You keep bringing your best every day, even if your best doesn't seem to be good enough. You're willing to come in early, stay late, get paid last, receive hard feedback and give things up for the good of the team. Something deep inside keeps you going when times are hard.

The sacrificial leaders we long to follow tap into something spiritual, something transcendent. A mentor of mine led a non-profit that has helped lift communities from poverty across the globe for decades. He's in his seventies, but he still sheds a tear when he talks about his work. I've watched him challenge leaders half his age over coffee and in boardrooms. He looks into our eyes and says, "If a leader doesn't have something that can bring them to tears in thirty seconds they're not truly alive."

The best leaders shape the future from their souls. They're anchored by deep beliefs they're willing to suffer for. They have an audacious optimism that dares to believe it can be different. The world celebrates Nelson Mandela now, but what kept him believing when he was in a South African prison? Martin Luther King Jr. is in history books now, but what kept him fighting for freedom through death threats? From our cozy movie chairs tears roll down our faces when leaders make great sacrifices or follow their values to the grave.

Sacrificial leadership comes from a deep place, but it must translate into practical realities. Soul-deep beliefs must turn into regular practices. This is where the rubber meets the road. If the deep beliefs and values below an organization aren't translated into practices they'll only live on the conference room wall and never in the stories of real people.

Effective coaching lives at the intersection of the spiritual and the practical. This is why I direct so much of my energy toward the practical things in the life of a leader and an organization. It's easy to say "family first", but when we send late night emails and ask leaders to work on the weekend we tell a different story. Many leaders didn't get practical training before they moved up the rungs of the ladder. Most leaders have to learn these skills as they climb. This is why coaching is so vital. This is why much of my best time goes to helping leaders with the practicals like scheduling, communication, meetings, boundaries, time blocking, collaboration and days off. Sky-high vision may be necessary, but culture is shaped five feet off the ground. Leaders are on the hook for applying organizational values personally and helping teams translate them into action. Great leaders translate values into practices. We live in a quick-fix culture, but the best stuff happens through repetition and dedication. Consistency breeds credibility.

The ripple effect

My therapist introduced me to a term called *limbic resonance*.[22] It describes the phenomenon that humans are constantly giving off signals to one another. We give off and pick up these signals unknowingly. If I'm off balance and spun up I transfer that "gift" to my son in the car when I pick him up from school or my coaching client during a session. If I'm joyful and fulfilled from the weekend that transfers to my team in our Monday morning meeting. We are all connected emotionally.

A leader carries extreme influence. If they are fearful or celebratory the room follows suit. Leader, you have way more influence than you think. You are a super spreader. Feels weighty, doesn't it? It's something every leader must steward well. Whenever someone tells me they don't have much influence I immediately disagree. Maybe they don't have millions of social media followers or a few hundred employees watching their every move, but they change a room when they walk into it. A person who does not comprehend their power is bound to wound people with it.

One leader I coached claimed he didn't have much influence in the company. I disagreed, of course, and we went to work on implementing his dreams for the company. Over a two year span, through intentional moves, he shifted the culture of the whole company through raising connection, personal excellence, accountability and systems. He proved himself wrong.

Every person has influence. Most leaders have five concentric circles of influence; ourselves, our family, our team, our organization and our community.

Ourselves. The change must start with us. Whatever we're experiencing personally we will reproduce to others. Changing any culture starts by first changing ourselves. I often take several deep breaths and pray a short prayer before walking into a new environment to make sure I'm grounded and grateful. Will you reproduce health or dysfunction, optimism or pessimism, hunger or apathy?

Our family. Our family feels the first effects of what we're experiencing. How we walk in the front door, or walk down the hallway from our office to the kitchen, shapes our families. The way a Mom or Dad carry themselves shapes the environment. It's hard to pretend at home. If work is chaotic and wearing us down we'll walk in amped up or threadbare. If we're energized they'll get the gift of our hope and energy. Designing a healthy, sustainable schedule and work environment is vital to showing up well for our families. Leaders often seek a coaching relationship when they are tired of bringing leftovers home to their family. Can you identify? I certainly can.

Our team. Those who work around us are directly impacted by our decisions and attitude. The boss shapes the meeting, but so does the person in the back of the room. When we enter grounded and prepared, communicate with kindness and lead with vulnerability we set a tone others will follow. When we disengage from the meeting texting on our phone or going off screen on Zoom we give permission for others to do the same. If we want our teams to be healthy, optimistic, aligned and trusting we must embody those. We carry the message within us, and we model the way forward. If you want to change your team make the changes in yourself first.

Our organization. We set cultural norms for our organization. I'll never forget how a friend lost trust in the CEO when he saw him parking next to a *No Parking* sign beside his office. This one small act signaled that it was okay for leaders at the top to bend the rules. People forget the company values on the wall, but they don't forget how we act. The higher a leader is on an organizational chart the more their actions will cascade through the entire organization.

Our community. We shape the dozens, hundreds or thousands of people around us. We are actively shaping our neighborhoods, co-working spaces, churches, social clubs and cities by how we choose to behave. Most leaders now shape an online community, as well. Leaders shape onlookers up close and at a distance. Two men in my community both own businesses, but have vastly different reputations; people have raved about one and warned me about the other. What will people say about you before you enter the room?

The three directional leader

I've never met a leader who didn't want to impact the present and the future. True innovation takes time and focus. It requires our constant attention and intention. Leading well for the long haul requires constant focus on three directions; looking back, looking within and looking ahead.

Execution; activating forward. Most leaders I encounter live in the future. They lay awake at night thinking about a world that doesn't exist. They're focused on problems to solve, goals to hit and dreams to actualize. This is necessary, but can be a burden to bear for them and others. They can be so focused on creating the future that they aren't living in the present.

Diagnosis; analyzing backward. When we study the past, our wins and losses can shape our future. We can gain awareness that shapes our action. Practices like checking in on goals, doing a post-mortem on failed projects or asking for feedback on how we are treating the team can be vital. Whether we succeeded or failed we can learn from the why and how.

Self-awareness and growth; cultivating inward. While the idea of self-awareness is en vogue, few leaders have practices to grow in self-awareness. Inward cultivation is vital for leaders to have a grounded identity. Many young leaders I encounter have a weak base; their triangle is tippy. As leaders strengthen the base their identity is more grounded and they become more resilient. One failure or critique doesn't throw them off. Developing the base allows leaders to look back at their past without something knocking them over. It also allows them to look to the future realizing they can risk failing without risking being a failure.

The Innovation Triangle

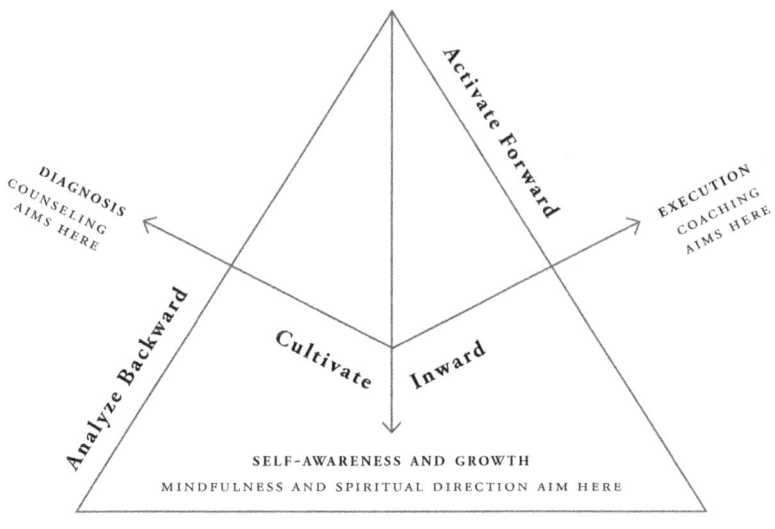

Which direction do you naturally lean?

What is good about that?

What is potentially unhealthy about that?

What direction is least natural for you?

What specific actions will you take to lean that direction?

Scan for tips on
using this tool

Anyone can lead well in one direction. The true challenge is leading ourselves and our teams in all three directions on a regular basis. We all lean one direction naturally. We must harness the power of our natural wiring while focusing on the other two directions. Practices are vital for living in these three directions. Without them we will over-compensate in one direction and accidentally avoid the other two.

I am naturally focused on the future. Strategizing and planning come easy to me. I have a corresponding weakness in looking back and analyzing how I got here. I often lose track of goals along the way or fail to analyze why something succeeded or failed. In order to curb my weakness I developed a quarterly audit and have honed it to help me overcome my weakness. The first time I did this I felt clumsy. It took too long and didn't bring the level of clarity I desired. Now I'm getting better at it and honing it each time. It's a skill, not a pill.

> **Reflect on your health**
>
> What is my greatest gap; humility, hunger, health or honesty?
>
> What are some specific ways I can bolster that area?
>
> What areas of unhealth in me or my organization concern me?
>
> Which direction do I naturally lean: backward, forward or inward?

THE TOPOGRAPHY
constant change

If we are going to succeed in this rapidly changing world,
we face two challenges:
making sense of the changes around us,
and making progress in an increasingly unfamiliar world
Dennis Holland

It was hard to process the range of emotions I was feeling. During a three day period I stood in the church Martin Luther King Jr. pastored, walked across the Edmund Pettus bridge in Selma where thousands began a march for freedom, looked up at 16th Street Baptist Church where a brutal bombing occurred and sat where Rosa Parks stepped onto a bus and changed history. It was a painful reminder of recent atrocities and a stunning marker of courage.

Throughout history a daring few have taken steps for what they believed, attracted others, shaped movements and changed societies. People have an amazing ability to envision and shape change, even in the midst of horrible realities. Change is never quick or easy, and movements never happen with one person.

This is a crucial moment in our culture. Massive change is unfolding in front of us in nearly every area of our lives. We're experiencing disruption in politics, the future of work, technology and our economic future. People are afraid. Loneliness and anxiety are at epidemic proportions. People can work from almost anywhere through our screens. Companies and workers are trying to figure out how this remote work thing can actually work. A.I. can generate instantly what was once painstaking.

> Change always creates fear and opportunity. Leaders tend to overestimate how much they like change, and underestimate how much energy change will require.

We've become a culture of outrage, yelling at a distance instead of pulling up a chair for a conversation. I'm committed to remaining a grounded optimist. We need catalysts who will galvanize unity, model civility and cultivate dignity. We desperately need healthy and whole leaders to light a path forward with lanterns of hope and optimism, not torches of fear and outrage. We need people who will steward power instead of abusing it.

It has never been easier for people to get a voice and use their voice. From social media to YouTube to writing platforms, ideas can spread like never before. This, of course, can be both good and bad. Those who speak up for good can get a voice, but it's also easy to create a raucous for evil. This is allowing longstanding injustices to come to light that were hidden for years from oppression to discrimination to scandals (thank goodness!). This has resulted in leaders being held to a higher standard of integrity and behavior.

Change always creates fear and opportunity. Leaders tend to overestimate how much they like change, and underestimate how much energy change will require. There are massive opportunities for those who are bold enough to shape the future. We must make sense of what is unfolding if we are going to make progress toward growth and healing.

PART ONE | Dispatches for the climb

Four postures toward change

There are four general postures toward change; *passive, adaptive, reactive* and *proactive*. Different changes impact us in different ways. No one is adaptive and proactive in every type change in every area of life, but once we are aware that we are reactive or passive toward a change we can take action and move toward being adaptive or proactive toward change.

The tool on the next page helps you to clarify how you process change. Write down three to five changes you anticipate or are already experiencing. Write them in one of the quadrants. Answer the accompanying questions in that quadrant. Then seek to move toward either the proactive or adaptive posture.

When the COVID 19 pandemic was simply "an issue across the world" I was passive about it. I thought it was ridiculous. I literally said, *"This may be a problem in China, but it will never cross our borders. Why are news stations blowing this out of proportion?"* I was quickly exposed as a fool. I moved into a reactive posture. Within a week I lost much of my income and professional momentum. I had no choice but to adapt and make necessary changes. When we move "through the center" of this process, as signified by the circle at the center of this tool, we have a heart shift. When I realized this would have a significant impact on the world I took action. Organizations that were proactive with this threat fared the best followed by those who adapted quickly.

Sometimes we're so afraid of obstacles that we're blinded to the opportunities. I have watched parents fear of the teenage years make them reactive with their kids. Julie and I aren't perfect parents, but we have thought proactively about the teen years. This has allowed us to provide meaningful experiences for our kids and try our best to "get ahead" of the teen years any way we could.

Change always presents obstacles and opportunities. When you look ahead and anticipate change you can shape the future through vision, not fear.

AntiBurnout

STAY FORTH: *POSTURES TOWARD CHANGE*

ADAPTIVE POSTURE:
DISCERNMENT
What is beneath this change?
How can we respond with wisdom?

PROACTIVE POSTURE:
PLANNING
What decisions must we make to
get ahead of this situation?

PASSIVE POSTURE:
APATHY
Why does change even matter?

REACTIVE POSTURE:
PROCRASTINATION
Can we wait to see if anything actually changes?

© Stay Forth Designs | Find more helpful tools at StayForth.com/resources

PART ONE | Dispatches for the climb

Reflect on change

What are the biggest changes I must process in my life or my industry?

What are some practical ways you can proactively lead the way through these changes?

What habits will help me remain optimistic amidst the fear of change?

THE ROUTE
your pathway up the mountain

Unsure of our direction we double our speed.
Unknown

The wind was beating us relentlessly with freezing rain as we climbed further up the valley. The peaks above us disappeared into the fog, and our shoulders were aching from the weight of our packs. We knew we would have to stop shy of our goal to make shelter, or hypothermia could quickly become an issue. My heart was pumping from the exertion, and my head with spinning with potential scenarios.

A team of four of us were in a remote valley of New Zealand's Southern Alps in the shadow of the country's highest peak, Mount Cook. Our team had only met the day before at the campground and officially charted our next adventure that night at the pub. We set our sights on ascending a world class peak the next week, but the first order of business was training. We needed to practice working together, upgrading our skills and learning the terrain. Our "practice run" was the most hairy mountaineering situation I had ever been in. I was doubting myself, my abilities and the brilliant idea we had over a pint the night before.

We yelled at one another through the whipping wind and freezing rain. We had no other options than screwing our tents to the smooth blue glacier below us. After battling to set up our tents we slid into our sleeping bags to warm up. We stayed in our tiny tents for two full days riding out the raging storm, struggling to stay warm and making warm meals. We woke up several times each night to the sound of ice avalanches raging down the nearby valleys. There was nothing fun about those two days of struggle. While this was the "practice expedition" it was also real. Eventually the clouds lifted, the sun rose and we trekked through green valleys and over rope bridges back to our basecamp.

Ten days later we stood atop Mount Aspiring with hands in the air hugging one another. It was the most beautiful view I've ever witnessed. After a twenty five mile slog through constant rain and flooded streams we threw off our packs. We were sore, utterly exhausted, soaked to the bone and glad to be alive.

Leaders who accomplish amazing things aren't the brightest; they're the ones daring enough to keep climbing. Leading requires vision for your climb, navigation of the route and resilience to keep going. You choose your mountain, chart the course and adapt your plan as you ascend. It's all real, but it's also practice.

The leadership pathway

Here is the pathway leaders must carve up the mountain.

Identify the peak. Decide on the peak you and your team are compelled to climb.

What is the goal we will accomplish?

Train for the peak. Learn the necessary skills to stay safe and climb the peak.

How must we prepare to reach our goal?

Decide on the route. Clarify the route up the mountain based on current conditions.

What is our strategy to accomplish this goal?

Climb the mountain. Start climbing the mountain and adjust the route as needed.

How will we stay on course? What adjustments must we make based on the conditions?
Recover for the next climb. Rest from the strain to climb another day. *How must we replenish our energy so we can take on another peak?*

Just like mountains have several possible routes, so do goals. Some paths are well-worn, others are rarely traveled. Conditions change, and we must adapt on the fly as new dangers arise. New routes present themselves. Just like the prophet Mike Tyson said, "Everyone's got a plan until you get punched in the face."

What mountain are you climbing?

Have you ever aimed at a big goal and been disappointed when you accomplished it? The feeling can wear off quickly. My friend used to call those "chocolate covered turds". Many people spend years identifying the peak they want to climb only to be empty and disappointed when they reach it. It wasn't enough.

We won't drift into the life we're designed to live. It only happens through intentional and proactive decisions. When you're identifying a peak make sure it truly matters to you. We must examine what it will cost us and how it impact the people we love most. Don't let professional goals rudder your whole life. Work is a piece of our lives, but was never meant to be the whole container of meaning. Make sure the mountain you start climbing is the one you want to summit.

Once you know the things that truly matter to you, the ones that are worth bleeding and sacrificing for, you can break them down into smaller goals that you can make progress on every week. We drift from our big goals. It's human nature. Great leaders keep big goals in front of them each week. What gets measured and celebrated gets done. We just have to make sure we're measuring the right things.

I want to invite you to consider a profound question; *"What is the good life for you and your family?"*[23] Not a decent life. Not a life others view as successful. A good life that is meaningful, fulfilling and aligns with what matters to us. A life like this, of course, is much bigger than our work. We can't cheat off someone else's paper here. The answer to this question is different for all of us, and it will determine our route up the ridges of the peaks we endeavor to climb.

My mentor, Jesus of Nazareth, is known for his teachings of love and compassion. He was a master question asker. When a man came to him for healing he asked a surprising and disarming question; *"What do you want me to do for you?"* He wanted to know what they wanted before he helped them, even if it seemed obvious. Isn't this what a great friend, coach or partner does? Asks questions about what we want without assuming?

Before working on goals with leaders I start by asking them to paint a picture of the good life. Their values, dreams and desires naturally leak out during this process. One leader may want to be great parent while another has a revenue goal that would lift the quality of life for their family or employees and another has the goal of retiring early and working in a non-profit. Others want a lifestyle of travel, time off work, adventure or flexibility to care for their aging family members. Our vision of "the good life" will determine the peaks we endeavor to climb, and the ones we don't. Leaders of depth think more about their eulogy than their year end reports. Pause to paint a picture of the good life a decade from now.

Impact goals and Identity goals

Most leaders have polarizing views of goals. Some leaders get excited as they head into goal planning season, others have sworn off formal goal setting. Some have a goal setting process that works well for them, but most haven't found that yet (but probably won't admit it). That was me for years. There are cracks in our traditional goal setting process.

We focus too much on visible professional goals and too little on invisible character goals. What good is it to hit our professional goals if our family is falling apart, our heart is empty, our body is wasting away and we're burning out?

We clarify our goals, but we don't clarify what we will invest to meet them. How can we set proper goals if we don't know the tradeoffs we're making?

PART ONE | Dispatches for the climb

We don't have a pathway to meet our goals, so they only remain as dreams.
What steps will I regularly take to reach these goals?

A healthier way to set goals
In light of these three cracks I worked to create a process for setting goals that synthesized two things; goals focused on who we are becoming below the surface and goals focused on what we do above the surface. Both matter, but we must connect them.

Every investment is based on delayed gratification; if we do small things along the way we will have more later. Anything you truly want is worth investing in. I've found investment language to be helpful when talking about goals.

Who I want to become; invisible roots. These are the things that are deep, relational, intimate, long-lasting and largely invisible.

Some examples: Relational connection with family and friends, culture goals, spiritual practices or health goals.

What I want to do; visible fruits. These are the things that can be easily counted and likely get celebrated by others.

Some examples: Revenue goals, new projects, organizational goals or a home purchase.

Invest about an hour on the Growth Game Plan on the next page. The leaders who invest in this process reference it years later.

Get moving
I've read and listened to a lot of books. In fact, I used to see it as a game. Each year I would set a number of books to read the next year. I would increase the goal a bit the next year and, of course, share the impressive final number on social media for the world to pat me on the back.

But most of this was foolish. I thought ingesting content would make me wiser. I read and listened to brilliant books, but I rarely translated them to my heart and hands. Many times I rushed through them and took no action steps. Zero. I gained some knowledge, but I didn't transfer that into wisdom. My life before and after the book or course or podcast or class or training looked the same. Have you ever

AntiBurnout

STAY FORTH: GROWTH GAME PLAN
A process to identify and invest in your dreams:

NAME _____

IMPACT DREAMS — What I want to do; visible fruits
IDENTITY DREAMS — Who I want to become; invisible roots

DREAM: _____
INVESTMENTS
- _____
- _____
- _____

DREAM: _____
INVESTMENTS
- _____
- _____
- _____

DREAM: _____
INVESTMENTS
- _____
- _____
- _____

DREAM: _____
INVESTMENTS
- _____
- _____
- _____

DREAM: _____
INVESTMENTS
- _____
- _____
- _____

DREAM: _____
INVESTMENTS
- _____
- _____
- _____

© Stay Forth Designs | Find more helpful tools at StayForth.com/resources

read a book, gone to a conference and filled out a workbook but never taken next steps? It's easy to become disillusioned about learning more, because we haven't seen any new results. Learning about how the body metabolizes fats and proteins is very different from going to the gym three times a week or changing your diet. The best principles only work if you do the work. If nothing changes, nothing changes.

After years of struggling to make big changes and guiding coaching clients through big changes I have found the following statements ring true.

New information alone does not yield transformation. If we're looking for change we have do more than ingest information. We must translate that knowledge into practice so it can change us and others around us.

> The best principles only work if you do the work. If nothing changes, nothing changes.

We are overwhelmed with information and hungry for experiences. We are exposed to so much information that it's paralyzing us. Many leaders believe they will change if they are constantly reading books and LinkedIn articles and consuming podcasts and courses. That can be a start, but transformation happens through next steps.

Breakthrough is found through new leadership skills, not leadership pills. We live in a culture of shortcuts. We're all looking for hacks to get where we're going faster. Sometimes there are no shortcuts; just new skills we need to learn. Skills take time to develop, and we will feel clumsy as we're learning them.

New awareness must lead to new action. Once we become aware of something it invites us into a new action. When we take this action we become aware of what we don't know and find more to learn. This cycle keeps us both hungry and humble as we grow.

The best leaders keep taking their next right steps. Knowledge without practice is only potential. Great leaders don't just take notes; they take steps. They try new things with what they've learned and experiment their way forward.

The books, talks and conversations that have changed my life soaked to my core. They messed with me, and informed my next steps (sometimes kicking and screaming). New awareness is only as good as the new actions we pair them with.

Perhaps the most impacting book in the last decade for me is *Why We Sleep*. In this book world renowned sleep specialist, Matthew Walker, shares almost anything you need to know about sleep. I was alarmed, perplexed, scared, inspired and challenged to change my life throughout this book. I listened to every word of this book, pausing the audio to take notes, write questions and declare next steps.

What was the context of my life? I read this during an exhausting time in my life and coaching career; the pandemic. Change was relentless. I had lost several coaching contracts due to the market conditions and leaders exiting their positions. I was working in a solo office with a decentralized team and looking through a zoom screen at most of my coaching clients. I needed to focus on both margin and sleep or I was only going to spiral into burnout.

What steps did I take? I focused on a consistent bed time and rise time every day. I put a napping couch and eye mask in my office, and began taking short naps almost every day. I made changes to aspects of my life that affect rest like exercise, diet, mental load and alcohol consumption.

What were the results? I began to catch lift about sixty days later. I felt more energy, settled into consistency with my sleep and my coaching excellence rose.

Matthew's research is impeccable and the content is world class, but apart from my actions this would have been fascinating information. Reading about sleep without making changes to my sleep would've done nothing.

Where the transformation happens

Confusion is paralyzing. The tool on the following page is a pathway toward change. Take about thirty minutes to work through the process. Identify one area you're currently confused about. Walk through the the process answering the questions and filling in the blanks. This is your first pass; aim for progress, not perfection.

PART ONE | Dispatches for the climb

STAY FORTH: *THE WHEEL OF TRANSFORMATION* | *A pathway from confusion to consistency*

CONFUSION: *IDENTIFY THE PRESENTING ISSUE*
What is confusing? / How will I find clarity?

CLARITY: *NAME THE REALITY UNDER THE ISSUE*
What has become clear about me? About this season? About this organization?

COURAGE: *TAKE THE NEXT STEP*
In light of this clarity what step must I take?

-
- When will I take this step?
-

CONSISTENCY: *DESIGN THE PROCESS*
What steps must I regularly take in this area?

-
-
-

When will I regularly take them?

-
-

COURAGE · CLARITY · CONSISTENCY

© Stay Forth Designs | Find more helpful tools at StayForth.com/resources

Spinning the Wheel of Transformation

This a simple process to follow when you're confused.

From confusion to clarity. When we're confused we can't take meaningful action; we must gain clarity. This process reveals what is going on beneath the issues and helps to identify a next step to take.

From clarity to courage. Taking a courageous step, even if it's small, gets us moving. Do it scared. Mark a date down and invite others to ask if you took it. Often that step loosens something and creates options. Movement creates energy.

From courage to consistency. The jump from courage to consistency involves translating a helpful action into a habit or practice. If a step you took was helpful take it regularly. Going to the gym the first time is great, but going regularly will change your life. When you schedule in that practice you have a continual pathway of movement and momentum. Regular rhythms are where true transformation is generated.

Consistency breeds credibility and creates momentum. This process can get you moving. Once things get moving they are easier to sustain. Your practices can be followed, tweaked and optimized for greater impact. Others may also begin to trust you more, because they see your commitment and results. This process can be applied to many areas of life; exercise, projects, sleep patterns, team meetings, parenting, spiritual practices and more.

> **Reflect on your route**
>
> What is the "the good life" for me and my family? Describe the various aspects in HD
>
> What are a few impact goals I am currently focused on?
>
> What are a few identity goals I need to refocus on?
>
> What culprits keep me from taking steps?

PART TWO
Obstacles and opportunities along the climb

> *The important work, the work we really want to do,*
> *doesn't come with a recipe.*
> Seth Godin[24]

It's no secret that this is a hard time to lead. We live in a demanding, entitled and outraged culture, and people direct plenty of that at leaders. We're processing heavy topics and seeking to lead others through them simultaneously. On any climb there are plenty of obstacles; raging rivers, loose rock, deep ravines and rock faces. The following obstacles cause leaders to lose sight of the peak and turn around on the leadership climb. But with every obstacle there is a corresponding opportunity through it.

THE OBSTACLE:
Overwhelm
THE OPPORTUNITY:
Clarity

When clarity goes up, overwhelm goes down

"You are carrying WAY more than you think!" I said this to Beth during a coaching session. If it wasn't enough to be directing a non-profit that empowers vulnerable women and children in Africa she was also running a family that required constant attention. I felt the weight of what she was carrying in her life and leadership through my computer screen.

I said the same thing to Steven. He had taken hits in every area of his life including his health while running an organization and showing up well for his family. I told John the same thing as he was trying to help his company evolve from a family-run joint into a fast-growing sustainable organization while caring for his team and creating steep goals.

Sometimes life is a LOT. It can hit us hard with no warning. Changes in our family, company, stage of life, team or health can bury us. Sometimes it feels like we're hiking up a muddy hill barefoot in the pouring rain; one step forward, three steps back. The weight of decisions, change, responsibilities and expectations can make us feel like we're going to crumble under the weight. Sometimes Atlas needs a shoulder massage.

Here are a few important things to realize about overwhelm.
Overwhelm is part of life and leadership, but we cannot stay here.
Overwhelm comes for all of us, but everyone responds to it differently.
Overwhelm can move from a feeling into a way of life if we do not take action.
Overwhelm, if not addressed, can slide into burnout.
Overwhelm can be a helpful signal you are carrying too much.
Overwhelm, if addressed wisely, can lead us toward helpful changes.

Sometimes what we don't know produces overwhelm. The fear of the gap can be greater than the obstacles we actually face. Brené Brown says, "In the absence of data, we will make up stories"[25] It's human nature, when we don't have the full story we assume the negative, not the positive. This is why relational connection and practices for building trust are vital to our teams. They build a relational bank of data that reminds us others are for us, not against us.

Sometimes we're overwhelmed because we've voluntarily taken on too much. Other times things were thrust upon us. Often it's a messy mix of both. Whatever the path that led you to overwhelm you cannot stay here. Prolonged overwhelm can slide into burnout. If you've felt overwhelmed for more than a few days it's time to attack the lie beneath it. There are two lies we tend to believe when we're overwhelmed; give up or grip for certainty.

Option 1: *Give up.* This flight response sounds something like, "What's the point? You're buried. There's no way to win or make progress. Quitting is your only option." This will lead to losing heart, giving up and surrendering forward movement.

Option 2: *Grip for certainty.* This fight response sounds something like, "You have to figure everything out. Find out every detail and white-knuckle your life with complete control". But this will lead you toward over-exertion and anxiety.

The third path; gain clarity. There's a middle path that begins by gaining clarity. The antidote for overwhelm is clarity. Instead of giving up or over-controlling slow down and ask, "What is overwhelming me?" Then you can get the struggle out of your head and on paper. Moving from confusion to clarity facilitates the great exchange where overwhelm decreases and clarity increases.

Clarity and overwhelm have an inverse relationship

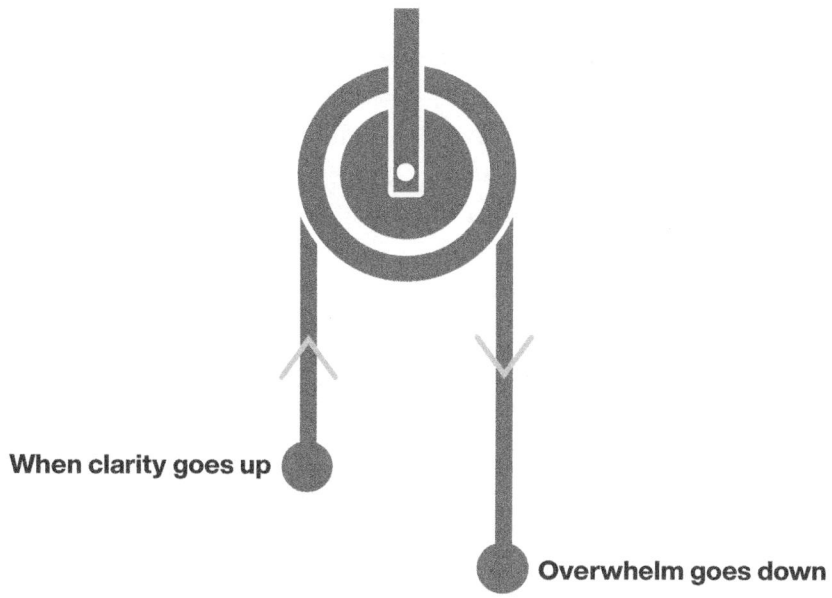

When clarity goes up

Overwhelm goes down

Clarity and overwhelm have an inverse relationship like this pulley system. If you can gain 5% clarity the overwhelm decreases at the same rate producing a 10% gain. Once you have clarity you can take steps out of overwhelm. Often, with a few steps, the problem untangles itself. In their book *Designing your Life* Bill Burnett and Dave Evans say, "You can't know where you are going until you know where you are"[26] Clarity helps us locate ourselves so we can cut a path through the underbrush of overwhelm toward healthy action.

When you're convincing yourself to grip for certainty (I call this over-control), remember, that is also a false narrative. Certainty is an illusion, and chasing it leads us further from health. Gaining clarity is possible, but finding certainty is not.

> Overwhelmed leaders create confusion, not focus.

We can't predict every detail we need to know. Where's your crystal ball that predicts the future? We don't just need clarity for ourselves; we need to cultivate it for those we lead. A 2018 survey of tech workers revealed the top cause of burnout was "Poor leadership and unclear direction"[27] Overwhelmed leaders create confusion, not focus. You cannot give what you do not have. If you want to create clarity you must find it first.

When we choose the middle path of gaining clarity we get ourselves ready for movement. Movement creates energy and momentum that gets us unstuck. When you feel overwhelmed you can pause, breathe and walk through this process.

Step 1: Identify the source of your overwhelm
Clarity questions: *What area/s of my life feels overwhelming? What aspects feel most overwhelming? Why?*

Step 2: Identify the lie you are believing
Clarity question: *What lie am I believing amidst my overwhelm?*

Step 3: Replace the lie with truth
Clarity question: *What truth can I replace that lie with?*

Step 4: Identify the step/s you will take.
Clarity question: *What actions can I take toward the area/s that feel overwhelming?*

Step 5: Take your next steps
Clarity question: *When will I take those steps?*

Step 6: Find allies to support you
Clarity question: *Who can support me in the process?*

PART TWO | Obstacles and opportunities along the climb

I often walk leaders through this process. At the end of a ninety minute coaching session the leader on the other side looks like a different person. They've identified where they were stuck, and their next steps. Their shoulders perk up, and they have a gleam in their eye. I love getting texts and emails letting me know they are moving forward.

Next time you're ready to give up or feel yourself grabbing for certainty take a few breaths, and remember there's a third way. Too much is at stake, and you'll only leave more issues for yourself and others to clean up later.

THE OBSTACLE:
Stuckness
THE OPPORTUNITY:
Newness

Getting unstuck requires us moving from a victim to a designer.

Ryan's email jumped out of my inbox. It was laced with urgency. He was ready to begin coaching immediately if, and only if, I believed I could help him navigate his vocational future. With full transparency he explained he was delivering solid results but he felt stuck inside a role, environment and organization that no longer suited him. He knew things needed to change fast!

During our second coaching session Ryan came to a massive realization; he had the ability to make many of the changes he desired. He didn't need to cross state lines or work for another organization. His vocational claustrophobia was largely an illusion. While he wasn't perfectly aligned with his current organization, he held the power to make many of the changes he desired. He worked hard to apply the tools between sessions, lifted the blame off the organization, and took responsibility for his life and leadership. His feet released from the mud.

AntiBurnout

Ryan's story is common. Many leaders are succeeding above the surface, but feel trapped below the surface. This can feel as terrifying as the walls closing in on you or as subtle as knowing you will have to create a new path in the future. Feeling stuck is exhausting and terrifying.

> When we stop growing we will find ourselves stuck in environments that no longer fit who we have become.

Our minds, bodies and hearts are designed for movement. Moving water nourishes life, stagnant water creates swamps. Hal Elrod, inspirational speaker and author of *The Miracle Morning* regularly says, "Movement creates energy". Healthcare professionals warn us, "Sitting is the new smoking". When we're tired after a long day it's tempting to sit and scroll. When we're not getting the results we wanted we're tempted to quit our disciplines. When we're tired of our lives we self-sabotage. We make bad decisions when we're sick and tired.

If you feel stuck you may not have anything broken in your life and leadership. Feeling stuck is a natural part of being a human, and taking responsibility for other humans. Emily and Amelia Nagoski, authors of *Burnout* say, "We may get stuck simply because we're constantly being exposed to situations that that activate emotion… No wonder 'helping professions' are so exhausted - you're confronted with people in need, all day, day after day."[28] If you keep seeking to serve others, challenge yourself and create change you will get stuck from time to time.

In fact, you may feel stuck because you have succeeded. Success can be even more disorienting than failure. Success breeds options and options produce disorientation. Sometimes we break our own barriers, and wonder, "What now?" Success often thrusts us into predicaments we've never faced before. The territory beyond success can be thick wilderness where every little noise sounds threatening and every step takes us further from civilization. I'm not sure who said it first, but "new levels, new devils" is the fitting phrase here.

When we stop growing we will find ourselves stuck in environments that no longer fit who we have become. We can be in a dysfunctional relationship, a boring job, an environment that is toxic (and I don't use that word lightly), responsibilities that feel over our head, bills that feel oppressive or a career field that seems to be going extinct. Like a plant that outgrows a pot or a fish that outgrows a tank sometimes we outgrow the environments we've existed in. And it feels disorienting.

Feeling stuck doesn't mean you're actually stuck. It may mean you are in "the land between." You have untapped potential and an untapped future, but you may not be sure how to get to the other side. Feeling stuck is a signal that more of the old isn't going to do. Your mind is telling you, "More of this cannot continue!"

When you're stuck you need to get moving. Movement requires six new things; mindset, options, actions, habits, environment and relationships.

A new mindset sheds stuckness. Our broken mindset is the number one saboteur of the life we desire. Our thinking can hold us back or propel us forward. These secret negative thoughts we carry weigh us down. If we want new results we need new thinking.

Thinking like a victim keeps us stuck[29]. There are, of course, true victims of atrocities in the world today, but in every atrocity there are examples of people who have done the brave inner work to move toward the future. They chose not to let a person or a situation define their whole lives. It's easy to stay stuck when you believe your life is determined by someone else. The victim mindset is everywhere! "Of course, it's everyone else's fault; the economy, the boss, the spouse, the company, the friends and the kids!" The victim mindset keeps creating a longer list of reasons the world is against us. It's easy to believe successful people are lucky and "the rest of us" are bound for struggle and failure. It takes the responsibility off of us, and leaves us safely stuck and wasting our best energy whining.

If you're thinking like a victim you'll need to shift to thinking like a designer. The designer bravely takes responsibility and journeys into the future. I'm not saying you don't have plenty of real obstacles pushing against you, but you can turn those obstacles into opportunities.

Victim thinking whispers, "I could never……" and "They're holding me back from…. ." Designer thinking ponders, "I wonder if I could....," and "What would have to be true in order to....?" Designers acknowledge the obstacles and devise a plan get to the opportunities. Life will never magically pause and become easy for more than a passing moment. God designed us with ability to take action and impact our environment. If you're in a terrible environment it may be time leave it and join another one or create another one.

> **Reflect on your mindset**
> What beliefs are broken, limited or outdated about my old mindset?
>
> What new beliefs can I replace them with?

New options shed stuckness. A new mindset produces new options. When we feel stuck there are only two options; this OR that. Beware of either/or thinking that limits your creativity and breeds tunnel vision. There are always more options than you think. When a coaching client feels stuck and is in this "the either/or tunnel" I have them work this prompt; "What would have to be true in order to _____ (desired result)?" This exercise often generates many options that lead toward the solution.

When we get tired we lose two things that spark our creativity; energy and optimism. But when new options appear curiosity can reappear with them. Don't judge or edit the options immediately; just ideate and spew them out. Later you can evaluate them.

> **Reflect on your options**
> What other options are possible?
>
> What would have to be true for these options to come to life?

New actions shed stuckness. It's hard to break bad habits without replacing them with better ones. Fast food is cheap, and it everywhere.

If you don't pack a lunch you're likely to end up with another bacon cheeseburger and fries. Scrolling is easy when you're tired, but an exciting new book could help you put the phone down. Drinking is easy when you're stressed, but a fun night with your kids can replace it.

In his book *Man's Search for Meaning*, concentration camp survivor and psychiatrist Viktor Frankl rebutted Sigmund Freud's thinking that man was driven by pleasure. He said that man was motivated by purpose, but sought pleasure in the absence of purpose. If he can direct his energy toward something meaningful like writing a best-selling book from a Nazi concentration camp how much more can we direct our energy toward something of purpose each day!

This is why it's vital to set goals that encompass both our life priorities and our professional goals[30] and review them regularly. If our goals are meaningful and top of mind we can direct our actions toward them. Today's writing session was a mini goal toward the larger goal of writing this book. I believe you will find freedom through the concepts in this book, and that keeps me going.

The best goals are worth sacrificing for. We take new steps because we know they matter. The human spirit is motivated by even the smallest slivers of progress. Break down your big goals into something smaller you can do every day and every week, then start moving. Don't wait until you feel motivated, start moving on your goals and you'll find motivation as you go.

> **Reflect on your actions**
> What actions are no longer helpful for the future I desire?
>
> What new actions or small goals can I replace them with?

New habits shed stuckness. New actions are helpful, but to produce long-term change they must sprout into habits. Healthy habits don't appear on accident and will always be met with resistance. Weeds grow in the garden quickly, but vegetables require careful cultivation.

I once wrote three books in three years. I don't recommend that to anyone, it was just how my story unfolded. It also happened to be the most full season of my life. My four kids were young, finances were low (okay, really low), and my work responsibilities were high. After realizing I would never be able to get away for a month in an A-frame cabin in the woods I carved out three hours each week to turn off my phone and write. Every Tuesday morning from 6-9 AM was my writing window. I sat at the same table of the same coffee shop drinking coffee from the same gray mug. I canceled everything during this block, and hit repeat every week. Three years later I had three books and a writing process that worked. More importantly, I didn't doubt I was a writer any longer; my habits told me I was.

> **Reflect on your habits**
> What actions do I need to translate into regular habits?
>
> When and how will I cultivate these habits each week?

New environments shed stuckness. We know instinctively that new environments produce new results. We naturally move to another spot in the office, the coworking space or the house to work on a different task. We go on a work trip and produce better things in a different place. New environments can spark freshness.

Author, pastor and dream cultivator Mark Batterson often shares a simple equation that can produce serious results.

Change of pace
+
Change of place
=
Change of perspective

If you want fresh thinking you may need to change your pace (or routine) and your place. Changing your environment can look like this.

PART TWO | Obstacles and opportunities along the climb

Blocking off a day a month to get out of the office to dream (try getting outside)
Planning recovery days after a big work push
Staying an extra day to dream or create at the end of a work trip or vacation
Going on that vacation you've been talking about
Working from the coffee shop one morning a week and getting out of your inbox
Taking your weekly or quarterly meetings offsite
Going on an anniversary getaway
Asking friends to swap houses in different states for a week
Getting into a coworking space three days a week and out of your home office

> **Reflect on your environment**
> What pieces of my work environment feel limiting?
>
> What changes in routine or location can I make?
>
> Where do I go to dream or be exposed to new ideas?

New relationships shed stuckness. Many times we get stuck in relationships that fit who we were, but no longer fit who we are becoming. These relationships can block us from cultivating new relationships with people who will take us to the next level. It takes guts to move on. I'm not telling you to ghost your old friends, but you may need to change how you interact with them. It's actually not their fault, it's no one's fault. It's a natural dynamic. I'm not saying I like this. I hate disappointing people! It feels like I'm giving up on them.

The extreme example of this is staying stuck inside a cult or an abusive relationship. We all wonder, "How can they choose to stay and put up with this!?!" But we all do it at a subtle level. We may not have to sneak out in the middle of the night in fear of losing everything we have, but we wonder how our decisions will impact what others think of us. "What will they think of me if I stop coming to their guys nights?" "Will they still seek my input on projects if we don't hang outside of work?" "If I stop showing up at this networking group will I lose business?"

Community has the power to shape us in healthy and dysfunctional ways. Who we are around shapes our mindset and our actions. When we let unhelpful voices influence us we normalize them. I've had to remove myself from negative groups, because I didn't want to think or act like them. Authors and thought leaders are relationships that influence us, too. I've stopped listening to podcasts and reading books that drove me toward extreme hustle and divisive thinking.

I had to make a major shift in my relationships about five years ago. I've always loved being accessible to local leaders and young entrepreneurs. I would drive all over town meeting with people. I began to get resentful when they would cancel on me, show up late or not take the advice they asked for. I had to realize it wasn't their problem; it was mine. I put myself in that position. I said yes to their request. As my priorities changed I began saying *no*, and directing them to more helpful environments where they could learn from others or in groups.

Freeing up this time and energy allowed me get into new relationships that stretched me. I joined a group of high capacity leaders seeking to remain healthy and grow their capacity. I began a group called Community Conversations with two friends at our coworking space to magnetize like-hearted leaders in our community. I had more space to seek out mentors. Maybe it's time to join a mastermind group, book club, CEO forum, or community group with people who will elevate you through osmosis.

> **Reflect on your relationships**
> What specific people or type of people are no longer helpful to who I am becoming?
>
> What specific people or type of people do I need around me in this season?

THE OBSTACLE:
Exhaustion
THE OPPORTUNITY:
Replenishment

Energy leaks effortlessly, but replenishment requires intentionality.

As a fun and relaxing summer comes to a close it's time for my family and I to ramp up for the challenges and opportunities of the fall. My kids head back to school, our schedules swell and my coaching clients need more challenge for the fall push. But one particular August I found myself exhausted. I wasn't ready for the regular fall climb.

The previous ten months piled on challenges in nearly every area of my life. We experienced life phase changes with our kids. A plumbing issue cascaded into a basement flood that resulted in a complete rebuild and an ongoing insurance battle. We had a bed bug infestation (it was really terrible, believe me) that limited our sleep every night. My wife had taken on increased responsibility in her work. I had partnered to launch a business that was requiring a lot my energy. These factors had slowly worn me down until I realized, "I'm exhausted. I cannot ramp up for the fall." I needed to find a process to replenish my energy.

We all get tired. It's part of being a human, a parent, a leader and a caregiver. But when we realize we're tired, we must make some changes or we won't be helpful for anyone around us. When we're tired, our judgment, energy and self-awareness are down. This blocks us from seeing just how tired we are. It's hard to create a wise plan to replenish when our energy is low.

We can be proactive to build in margin before we get to a spot of exhaustion. Author and professor Cal Newport says, "Downtime helps recharge the energy needed to work deeply."[31] Finding downtime in a world that is always "on" will require constant resistance. Think about it; our culture of over-stimulation, over-commitment and over-promising has a gravitational pull toward a tiredness cycle. We live in a culture of excess and efficiency that celebrates getting more and doing more in less time. This "more, more, more mentality" sucks us toward an exhaustion cycle where we can feel trapped inside of our own life. Throw some change in your family, your home, your health or your work and you can tank quickly.

When we feel overwhelmed or behind we tend to follow our biology into two responses: fight or flight.

Flight. In flight mode, we avoid what we need to do. Things at home, work or both pile up on us and it feels overwhelming. In fight mode we often stay busy in order to numb ourselves. It can be as blatant as addiction or subtle as distraction.

Fight. In fight mode, we work harder, adding hours to our already already full schedule thinking this will dig us out. We often abuse or over-use caffeine and adrenaline keeping us hyped up, and limiting our sleep. This leaves us pushing too hard for too long without times for our body to "come down" and rest. We know if we rest for long we're likely to crash. So we just keep going.

Many leaders are living a combination of fight mode and flight mode. This looks like getting revved up, staying revved up and eventually crashing. I've lived in this "push hard and crash cycle" many times. In fact, I didn't know there was another way to live for a long time. I thought that's what good leaders did.

No matter how proactive you are tiring moments and seasons will sneak up on you like they have for me. Pain, life circumstances and

PART TWO | Obstacles and opportunities along the climb

responsibilities are part of the human experience, and you are, after all, a human. Here are four steps to take when you're unusually tired

Step 1: Assess the level of your tiredness

Not all tiredness is created equal. As a coach, I want to understand the level of tiredness the leader is experiencing. Look for these three types of fatigue.

Expected fatigue. You've been running hard for a relatively short time (six months or less), and this fatigue was expected. You have a timeline and an actual plan to slow down. As long as you have a true time of rest coming and a shift to your routines replenishment is on the way.

Extended fatigue. You've been running hard for an extended time (more than six months) and you have no plan to reverse this. It may be mysterious to you. You may wonder, "Why am I SO tired?" This is dangerous, especially if you have no plan to slow down or a plan to replenish. It's time to develop a reversal plan.

Extreme fatigue. In this zone you're heading toward burnout. You've lost desire to do a lot of the things you love (ironically those things can help you replenish), and you've accepted realities of your fatigue as normal for far too long. You may have real and pressing reasons for this like young children or family medical issues. You don't know how to reverse this, and you're not sure you have the energy, anyway. You are experiencing numbness in many areas, and you could be experiencing depression, also.

If you are in extended fatigue or extreme fatigue, I recommend going to the doctor to get bloodwork done. There may be an underlying medical issue. I also recommend good therapy to identify the root causes of your overwork or over-extension.

Assess the level: *What is my level of tiredness: expected fatigue, extended fatigue or extreme fatigue?*

Step 2: Assess the source of your tiredness

In order to make changes you'll need to evaluate which aspect of your life is most tiring. Don't just think about work and home, it's more nuanced than that. Here is a helpful grid.

Body. Your physical body is worn down. Common causes can be lack of sleep, lack of exercise, bad eating habits or a lack of margin.

Mind. Your mind is overextended. Common causes can be screen habits, working in the evenings, leading in too many areas, work that tilts away from your unique design, too many decisions, and pervasive change.

Relationships. Your relationships are a source of constant stress and conflict. Common causes can be people who take from you but don't give back, ongoing low-grade conflict or family drama.

Heart. You have experienced significant loss and may not have had space or a process to grieve it. Common causes can be major changes personally or professionally, painful incidents you haven't dealt with or hopelessness in a certain area.

Soul. You have had tectonic shifts in your identity, faith or family. Common causes can be lack of purpose, a faith crisis or the loss of a job that was connected to your identity.

It's often combination of these areas, but try to pinpoint one area that hurts more than the rest.

Assess the source: *Which area of my life is the greatest source of tiredness right now? Why?*

Step 3: Make changes to reverse the cycle

> We've undervalued and under-understood the power of rest

Regardless of your tiredness level, you must take action. The moment we're "sick and tired of being sick and tired" is a key moment to create a plan to reverse the cycle. In extreme cases you can take time for an extended break, but this is rarely an option last minute.

We've undervalued and under-understood the power of rest. Rest is not just getting your sweatpants on and sitting on the couch. Physician Saundra Dalton-Smith has identified seven types of rest: physical rest, mental rest, emotional rest, spiritual rest, social rest, sensory rest, and creative rest[32]. Each type of rest can bring replenishment to a particular flavor of strain. Our narrow view of rest limits our replenishment. We've skipped over certain things that don't "count" as rest that could actually replenish us deeply. The flavor of your fatigue should shape the flavor or your rest.

If the currency of leadership is energy, not time, we must evaluate our energy carefully. Each person is unique. In order to reverse our energy drains we must be aware of them. We must also know what fills us.

Drains. These are things that take energy from us. They go against the grain of who we are. While we can't avoid all of these in our home and work, we can be aware of them and limit them. Your "Drains List" should cover personal and professional items.

Fills. These are things that lift your energy and your spirit. These big or small things enliven you and get you going. Your "Fills List" should also cover personal and professional items. Once you are aware of them you can practice them regularly. Be as specific as possible.

MY DRAINS	MY FILLS

For most people getting outside is a massive fill. Tim Keller famously said, "Beauty heals the soul." In our screen-heavy world the serenity and beauty of the outdoors can truly heal us. So can art, beautiful spaces and meaningful relationships.

When I need to replenish, I instinctively seek out beauty. I'm drawn to Creation and community. I go downtown to interact with people, and I go to creation to see unspoiled beauty. I live in the median space, the suburbs, between these two spaces of beauty. Beauty is always important, but never urgent.

Once you identify the level and source of your tiredness you can create a plan for what you will START doing, STOP doing and KEEP doing to reverse the tiredness cycle. I modified a popular tool called "Start Stop Keep." It can be very effective in creating a reversal plan for your exhaustion. Just filling this tool in won't change your life; you have to act on the life and leadership commitments every week. I challenge you to put them directly in your calendar on repeat.

Make changes: *What do I need to START, STOP and KEEP doing? When will I quit or repeat each of these?*

Step 4: Cultivate a regular replenishment cycle

We started by gaining awareness of the level and source of your tiredness. Then you made commitments to remove the things that drain your energy and repeat the things that give you energy. But in order to create ongoing replenishment you must create habits that help you replenish regularly. An annual vacation is not enough to sustain the rigors of navigating our culture, caring for our family and doing meaningful work week after week.

Energy leaks effortlessly, but replenishment requires intentionality. If you don't calendar your replenishing activities and turn them into habits urgent matters will eat them up. When habits slip it's easy to slide back into a tiredness cycle. Habits are ten dollar investments that give ten thousand dollar returns. You may experience small gains quickly from your habits, but expect sixty days of practicing your new habits before you see any serious lift. That's how investing works.

PART TWO | Obstacles and opportunities along the climb

STAY FORTH DESIGNS: START, STOP and KEEP

NAME _____

STOP DOING: *What is eroding my health and impact that I need to stop doing immediately?*

1. _____ WHY: _____
2. _____ WHY: _____
3. _____ WHY: _____

START DOING: *What can I start doing immediately to increase health and impact?*

1. _____ WHY: _____
2. _____ WHY: _____
3. _____ WHY: _____

KEEP DOING: *What is producing fruit that I should continue doing?*

1. _____ WHY: _____
2. _____ WHY: _____
3. _____ WHY: _____

DESIRE TO STOP DOING: *What do I desire to stop doing eventually that is currently necessary?*

1. _____ WHEN: _____
2. _____ WHEN: _____
3. _____ WHEN: _____

DESIRE TO START DOING: *What do I desire to start doing eventually that is currently unrealistic?*

1. _____ WHEN: _____
2. _____ WHEN: _____
3. _____ WHEN: _____

© Stay Forth Designs | Find more helpful tools at StayForth.com/resources

Here are a few guideposts for creating replenishing habits.

Plan for the long haul. As Steven Covey says; "Begin with the end in mind."[33] As you plan your habits think about what you can sustain for an extended period of time.

Focus small. Habits compound. When you take small steps you prove to yourself you have what it takes. Keep collecting small wins like compounding interest.

Repeat them regularly. When you know the steps you're going to take put them on your calendar, as if they're a vital meeting or task. Because they are. The more often you repeat these replenishing habits the more energy you'll get. Make them automatic and easy to repeat. Momentum and routine are your friend. Capitalize on the momentum of small wins, and seek to transfer that to other areas.

Raise your commitment as you go. When it comes to growth I'm a fan of evolution, not revolution. As you stack your wins you can increase them slowly as you and your schedule are ready. Starting with huge commitments can lead to discouragement and quitting, like most New Years resolutions.

Daily habits for replenishment

Here are examples of replenishing habits that require only 10-30 minutes a day.

Walk one mile (approximately 20 minutes)
Pray or meditate
Pack a healthy lunch
Plan your day first thing each morning (use our Right Side up Journal for this)
Take a short nap a few times a week (20-35 minutes actually helps)
Step outside in the sun between meetings
Journal about your day each evening
Get a quick work out or run
Eat lunch with your coworkers
Get to bed at a specific time
Listen to a nourishing book or podcast
Create something with your hands
Call a friend on the way home from work

Write an encouraging note
Drink half your body weight in water ounces

Weekly habits for replenishment
Here are examples of replenishing habits that can help you each week.
Set aside a weekly sabbath day to pause from all work
Designate a fun family night
Block off a 2-4 hour chunk for creating
Get extended time in the outdoors
Spend a few hours with friends who encourage you
Sleep in one day a week
Work from another location one day, morning or afternoon each week
Create a weekly date night with your spouse or children
Come home early on Fridays
Do an activity you love and look forward to

These are examples that work well for others. You can borrow from others, but be careful not to set others habits as your gold standard. Here are a few habits that have been huge for me over the years.

Sunday planning session. My wife and I meet for about thirty minutes on Sunday evening to plan for the upcoming week and month. We coordinate rides, talk about unique circumstances, make decisions on invitations and look ahead for breaks we can take.

Regular hydration. I heard an estimate that 70% of Americans are constantly dehydrated. It takes constant work to stay hydrated, but creates sharpness and limits snacking.

Appropriate sleep. I have a set bedtime and wake time each workday. I also take short naps (20-35 minutes) throughout the week, and have a day to sleep in each week.

Varied exercise. I do a combination of efficient gym workouts, runs with my dog, intense trail runs and daily walks. I need to vary my exercise in this season of life and stay moldable to our changing family schedule.

"To Don't list." I love being with people, so I need constant focus on saying no to good opportunities that aren't the best opportunities.

My "to don't list" has been helpful for me to avoid over-scheduling and over-committing. Making these decisions ahead of time (for me this is Sunday afternoon) helps to limit options before a pressurized moment occurs.

Your unique wiring

Have you ever tried to do something that worked for others and it completely bombed? The thing that brings others life and effectiveness may be a complete waste of your time. We're all put together differently. Understanding our unique wiring is vital to leading well for the long haul. Here are a few important areas to evaluate how your unique wiring will impact your replenishment cycle.

Chronotype. This refers to when you do your best work. In his book *When*, Dan Pink highlights three type of people. Larks generally do their best work in the early mornings, owls generally do their best work in the evening or late night and "third birds" are somewhere in between[34]. Once you understand your chronotype you can schedule your responsibilities during your optimal time.

Introvert or extrovert. A large number of leaders mistakenly believe they are extroverts, because their job requires them to be with and inspire people. I view introversion or extroversion describing how you recharge. Introverts recharge by being alone, while extroverts recharge by being with people. This is not whether you like being with people or are good with people, but how you recharge. Once you know this you can plan spaces to recharge with or away from people proactively.

Your learning style. Many leaders don't know how they learn best. Are you auditory, visual, experiential, tactile or kinesthetic? This will shape how you take in information and iterate your work. I am a kinesthetic learner, so if I feel stuck I get moving on a walk or a run, and it generally loosens something up. I'm also visual so I try to create diagrams and sketches to cement my learning.

Seasons of momentum and rest. It's important to understand the rhythm of your year and recognize the season you are in. If you know what season you are in you can have appropriate expectations and schedule appropriate activities for that season. A momentum season is very different from a rest season, but we need both. Be careful not to compare your seasons to others. Your family and profession may have unique energy peaks and troughs. Some leaders are wired to thrive in momentum seasons, others seem to thrive in calmer seasons. Know your strengths and limitations here.

The Obstacle: Change
The Opportunity: Experimentation

Experiments test the future without pressurizing it.

I was curled up in a fetal ball under a weighted blanket. It was 5:30 PM, and I had barely survived the workday. It felt like I had three hundred pounds pushing down on my chest. I had never experienced something like this before. "What's happening? Is this a panic attack?"

Something was very wrong. I had always been energized by work. I looked forward to each day, anticipating the people I would invest in, the problems I would solve, the content I would design and the new things I would bring to life with my team. Instead, I was scared and exhausted.

I desperately wanted to invest my best energy helping leaders navigate their path through coaching, consulting and creating content, but I was afraid. Afraid of failing. Afraid of looking like a fool. Afraid of not being able to support my family. I was about to gain a lot and lose a lot simultaneously.

That intense season and my "fetal ball moment" was a tipping point that helped me make my jump into coaching full-time. It was terrible, but it was necessary. We must go through terrifying and painful moments to get where we're going. They forge who we are, and shape who we're becoming. They are like the bear hunt in one of my favorite childrens books.

We're going on a bear hunt
Can't go over it
Can't go under it...
Just going to have to go through it[35]

I often repeat these words to leaders when they're about to make a big move. Our minds are always trying to invent ways to go over or under the next challenge instead of going through it.

> Above the surface of the change there is freshness, and below the surface there is pain.

Change is always accompanied by turmoil. I've walked closely with leaders through shifts like having their first child, resigning from a job they've outgrown, moving across the country, launching their last child out of the nest, transitioning into the CEO role, selling a company, burying a parent and navigating midlife. All these changes bring excitement, and pain. Above the surface of the change there is freshness, and below the surface there is pain. When tectonic plates shift in our heart, mind and future, hot magma is boiling below the surface. We must attend to these hotspots or they can spew great damage upon us and others.

You cannot shape the future without change. Change brings loss, and loss creates fear. You can't go over, around or under change; you've got to go through it. If you resist change you will seek to return to a past that no longer exists.

Forward-thinking leaders (me included) can think they are immune to pain of change. We fancy ourselves as good at change and skilled at navigating the future. We escape boredom or the pain of the present moment by escaping to the future. We declare war on the status quo through aggressive goal setting and bold declarations of what we'll

PART TWO | Obstacles and opportunities along the climb

accomplish. And we think we can just skip the pain, the loss and the grief.

I have never regretted launching Stay Forth, but it has been more painful than I imagined. I have had to change my mindset and methods many times. I only wish I had a coach to walk through the launch season with me. I wish someone would've grabbed me by the shoulders and said, "Alan, you need to grieve everything you are losing, so you have space to hold everything you're gaining." It's been brutiful; brutal and beautiful.

I wish I could skip this section. But I can't. If you want to influence people toward things that are good, true and beautiful you'll have to get comfortable navigating change. Before we can change the world we must change ourselves. If I'm guiding you on a backpacking trip in the Rockies, I can help you pack the right gear, create shelter, and carry the right food. But I can't carry you up the grueling steps with your lungs burning at high altitude. I hope this section can help you lighten what you're carrying in your leadership pack.

Let me take some pressure off; you're not supposed to know everything about what you're doing. If you do you need a new challenge. Let me go a step further. We are making this up as we go. We may use cute words like "adapting," "innovating" or "pivoting," but we're learning on the fly. Making it up as you go is part of leading in this fast-paced age.

The antidote to change is experimentation. In fact, experiments are how we are going to get the info we need to move forward.

Why are experiments helpful?

They limit the pressure and increase our curiosity
They open our mind to new possibilities
They give us data to innovate and make future decisions
They free us and our team to make mistakes
They put us in learning mode and heighten our senses
They move us toward the future when we're stuck
They help us stumble on new ideas

Experiments are for learning, not winning. The learning IS the win. If you can label a risk "an experiment" you can take the pressure off succeeding. Phrases like "let's try this and see what we can learn" engage our curiosity and evoke bravery.

I watch a lot of leaders load up expectations when launching new things by expecting everything to work. They believe every little piece of the product has to work. They brand the new program, share what the outcomes will be, and guarantee success to investors. They expect the new hire to produce immediate results. When it doesn't turn out that way it feels like failure instead of learning.

I've done this, too. I once hosted a book group that bombed. The reason it was painful is because it was my book. I put way too much work into making sure it worked and would validate my work. It felt personal, like no one showing up to your kid's first birthday party. It should've been an experiment. I could've saved a lot of time and pain.

The Obstacle: Pain
The Opportunity: Connection

Leaders need good therapists, skilled coaches and wise mentors,
but most of all leaders need friends.

I used to rock climb regularly. It was one of the greatest distractions of my life. My buddies and I could disappear into a different world for a few hours. Not only were the towering red cliffs of Garden of the Gods a kind of Eden escape, but climbing required my full attention. When I was climbing, nothing mattered except getting to the next hold, the next bolt and the top of the climb.

Sometimes I would fall a few feet (or more) before my belayer pulled me tight and the rope would stretch and catch me. It's an incredible feeling when the rope catches you! In all the falls I took (and there were plenty) I never felt immediate pain. The adrenaline was pumping too hard. But I would often look down at my arm or leg when I was safely back on the ground to see a bloody gash. One time I climbed hard for hours after a fall, but could barely limp to my car when we finished. Climbing forced such intense focus that I had no idea when I was hurt. The adrenaline and focus masked the pain. This is the life of many focused leaders. They are so focused on the activity of the moment they have no idea how much pain they are carrying.

Leaders are "the walking wounded", the "wounded healers."[36] This is especially true of those in helping professions. Many times leaders sustain intense personal and organizational pain simultaneously. Often they see no other choice than to just keep leading through it.

> Pain is part of being a human, so pain is part of being a leader. The more people you influence the more pain you'll be exposed to.

Their family needs their presence and the paycheck. Their employees need to know the company has a future after the big layoffs. Congregants need healing after the church split. The executive team needs stability and optimism when they're hemorrhaging finances and credibility after the scandal. In moments of pain, people look for leaders. But the leader has been hit hard, also, sometimes even harder than the rest.

I understand every leader can't take a long vacation after a crisis, but at some point you must make space to pause. Often crisis causes leaders to run even harder. Perhaps they know how painful this experience will be to unpack so they try to outrun their pain. we are especially gifted at staying busy to avoid pain.

Pause and think about the hardest thing you've been through as a leader. Perhaps it unfolded in a moment or perhaps it was a long, painful season. Take five deep breaths and close your eyes.

What was the hardest part of that experience or season?
Who have I processed that experience with?
How much anger and fear do I still carry from that experience?

Let's start with the bad news. **Pain is part of being a human, so pain is part of being a leader. The more people you influence the more pain** you'll be exposed to. It's painful to trust again. If not dealt with, pain can multiply into more pain. It can turn you bitter, cynical, cold, withholding or angry.

You know the adage, "Hurt people hurt people?" It's especially true of leaders. Remember, leaders have inordinate amounts of influence on others. Brené Brown says, "Pain that is denied or ignored becomes fear or hate."[37] Our culture has plenty of fear and hate, which makes me believe we have a lot of unprocessed pain from parents, people next door, and presidents. Young Adolf Hitler wanted to be a professional artist. Can you imagine how the world would be different today if he would've created masterpieces instead of genocide?

If you don't process your pain in healthy outlets it will become a burden for you and a curse to others. The pain you carry can debilitate you or transform you. Maybe you don't have outright anger, but you disguise your pain as cynicism. This is more harmful than you can imagine. Cynicism blocks our ability to hope things can be different and disconnects us from people physically, emotionally, or both.

But there's good news. When we do the hard work of processing pain it can be transformed into a gift. Pain can bloom into gratitude, empathy and perspective. Then we can offer these as gifts to others. This is why it's so inspiring when those with serious disabilities or massive losses choose joy and hope instead of bitterness and cynicism. People who have experienced atrocities have more reason to complain than we ever will. Processed pain reminds us what matters to us, connects us to others and gives us clues on how to move forward in a wiser way.

Pain isn't the focus of this book, but identifying our pain can lead us toward health and healing. While there are plenty reasons for pain in leadership I will share the big ones I see most commonly.

The pain of loss — when something or someone close to you is gone. Loss sneaks up on leaders, especially visionary leaders. Loss is the necessary bi-product of change. You can't get change without loss. Leaders are in the change business, which means we'll need to become good friends with loss. Visionary leaders live in the future and often forget to look back at the past or become aware of the pain they are carrying.

Loss doesn't always leave gaping holes, sometimes it leaves microscopic shrapnel.

These situations create micro-losses.

Moving on from a season of the organization that was simple or fun

A teammate you loved moving to another team or division

Changing a routine that you loved

Elevating to a new layer of leadership and losing the simplicity of the last role

New owners taking over the company

Peering at future that looks very different from the past

Kids moving over a milestone

The pain of rejection — people distancing themselves from you or exiting your orbit. It's painful when a volunteer or staff member leaves the organization. Even if we rationally understand their move to another organization, division or across the country is "a good move for them," we can still feel abandoned. It can feel personal to us, but "it's just business" to them. We can even feel rejected if no one picked our idea, took our advice, chose us for that project, included us on the email for feedback, picked someone else for the promotion, or invited us to happy hour.

I had to fight off feelings of abandonment when a teammate moved to another state for great reasons. I fully supported their decision, but they left a crater behind them. I was left with more responsibility, and I lost a friend.

Pain signals the need for connection. When my kids slam their hand in the door or break up with their boyfriend they run to my wife and I immediately. They understand innately the antidote for pain is connection. Or reconnection. Many people feel they have nowhere to run. David Brooks says, "Our society suffers from a crisis of connection".[38] The future we idealize drives leaders to stand alone and push through the pain. But isolation blocks healing and multiplies pain. To complicate things we're often running so fast we may not even realize we've experienced pain.

We heal in relationships. We crave connection from the womb to the tomb. It literally helps minds, hearts and bodies heal. Medical researchers observed patients after a heart surgery and saw two major factors that brought healing after the surgery. "Being socially supported and taking comfort in your faith makes you seven times more likely to survive major heart surgery than someone who has neither of those things in their life."[39] The patients who had connection to the Divine and to a community healed at a much higher rate. Their conclusion; "People thrive when they feel loved and languish when they don't."[40]

Leaders need friends. We all need safe spaces to grieve losses and celebrate wins. Over the last decade I've witnessed the rise of what I call "loser communities." These are spaces where it is only okay to be struggling and never okay to be winning. Perhaps these spaces are a pendulum swing from the spaces where everyone seems to give the vibe "I'm killin' it!" Loser communities attract people, but they become a black hole. If you are only safe to share your losses, but you cannot celebrate your wins, it's not a community; it's a den of victims.

So, where can leaders go to engage their pain? Here are four healthy places.

Friends can help you grieve and celebrate

Leaders carry a power dynamic if they control outcomes or have influence over others paycheck. This can leave leaders feeling like everyone wants something from them all the time and questioning who their true friends are. Leaders need friends — people who aren't impressed by them, and don't need anything from them. When we're with a friend we can vent freely about the situation without wondering if we've shared too much or worrying that we'll get canceled.

Friends can be especially helpful as another source to air out their pain besides their spouse. While we should be transparent with our spouses, this often becomes a large burden for them to bear and can impact their view of our team. Often the spouse carries this pain deeper and longer than the one who was hurt. Friends don't have to understand your industry to help you process your pain.

Caution about friends: Make sure not to just view your friends as a dumping ground for your pain, or they won't be excited to hang on a Friday night. Make sure you don't accidentally create a "loser community" where it's only okay to be hurting and never okay to be winning. Also, be wise with what you share as it will impact relationships.

Therapists can help you identify and process your pain

I'm a big fan of good therapists. They can bring an objective view of our pain and offer valuable tools to help us face our pain. In one season of my parenting, I had no more tools to understand one of my kids. I knew my perspective was limited. I didn't want to damage our relationship, so I sought out a therapist. He helped me understand myself, my pain, and my kids and move toward connection with them. That investment of time and money will impact our family for a long time.

It's helpful to have a chemistry fit with a therapist. Don't give up if you don't get the right fit the first few times; it only takes one. Ask friends for a recommendation. In some places there is still a stigma about seeking a therapist. If we want to change this stigma we need to take the first steps to normalize therapy. Referencing your therapy journey can give others permission to seek therapy for healing as well.

Caution about therapists: For most, therapy shouldn't be forever. When you and those around you believe you've found perspective and healing you can move on or take a break. Don't use therapy as a way to stay stuck instead of a way to heal.

Coaches can help you elevate your health and performance

A great coach who understands the challenges of your work can help you transfer confusion into movement. My clients often show up to a coaching session stuck, and ninety minutes later they have clarity on next steps and the confidence to take them. I listen and acknowledge their pain, but the goal is healthy movement into the future. Alignment and experience are vital. Most coaches offer a free session to assess your obstacles and opportunities. During this session pay close attention to the chemistry you have and listen for their experience. Many of the best coaches don't have the certifications and education but have an ability to connect and valuable experience.

Caution about coaches: There are good coaches and bad coaches. There are also coaches who understand the weight you carry and those who don't. Your coach can only help you take ground if you're honest. If you're not continuing to take ground with your coach you may be done with the engagement. The best coaches help you uncover clarity, unearth your greatness and get out of the way.

Fellow strugglers can help you normalize

Intentionally guided groups like mastermind groups, executive groups or leader pods can be powerful. Often leaders gather with others who feel a similar weight of leading and find healing and community. When I host these groups the apex of our time are often the adventures, the laughs, the tears, the new experiences, and the in-between spaces where leaders accidentally bond. While you may feel like a freak in other places, these groups can turn beautifully into a "freaks like me" club. There's a magic when we find out there are others we can identify with.

Caution about fellow strugglers: Sometimes you get bad advice in these spaces. Make sure to separate others baggage, opinions and advice from your situation. Some peer coaching moments can lead you astray. There is a time to seek a professional.

The Obstacle: Disappointment
The Opportunity: Naming

Disappointment is always a product of unmet expectations. When we "name the gap" between what we expected and what we got we can move forward.

While disappointment is a form of pain, it's worth a whole section. It stacks up on leaders eroding their hope. Disappointment is always a product of unmet expectations. When you get less from yourself, the circumstance or others, than you expected disappointment is the result. Disappointment can be big or small, external or internal, realized or unrealized. Brené Brown says, "The more significant the expectations, the more significant the disappointment."[41]. When we hope big we can hurt big.

Internal disappointment. You can be disappointed in yourself that you didn't react better, wake up earlier, work harder, seize the moment or get the promotion.

External disappointment. You can be disappointed that your friend didn't read that book you gave them, that a group canceled you after "the incident", that no one remembered your birthday, or that your business closed.

> Naming expectations proactively is the easiest way to avoid disappointing others later.

The antidote to disappointment is naming the gap between what you expected and what you got. In order to move forward from disappointment we must become aware of the difference between what we expected and what we received. Whether you missed a fundraising goal, didn't get the job or failed to lose weight on the diet, naming the gap is vital to clarity, courage, and healing.

Do any of these internal thoughts or statements sound familiar?

"I thought I would be THERE by now!"

"Why am I still struggling with this?"

"I thought the company would at least _____ after I served them so well."

"I thought _____ would lead to _____."

"Why haven't you _____ yet?"

Named expectations are things you clearly aimed at and missed. Unnamed expectations are desires you didn't know you or others had until they weren't met. Brené Brown calls these "stealth expectations"[42] Sometimes I'm speechless when people share their disappointments with me. I had no idea what they desired from me until disappointment showed up in a stealthy way.

I've become a big fan of naming expectations early and clearly. I'd rather avoid the pain of stealth expectations shanking me. Naming expectations proactively is the easiest way to avoid disappointing others later. Leaders, we are never as clear as we think. Sometimes we honestly forget the number, date, promise or wording we told others. I always encourage leaders to write things down and send them to the other person, especially after a conversation where emotions are high.

Frustration is disappointment with an edge. Most leaders say, "I'm not angry; I'm frustrated. Yeah, sure. I've said this, too. Little frustrations at ourselves and others can build up until we explode or pull away. Address frustrations early and head on or they will weigh on you and eventually escape publicly. Instead of addressing our frustrations we joke about them passive-aggressively. Pay attention to what you pay attention to; the weight of frustrations and disappointments compounds.

The Obstacle: Resistance
The Opportunity: Movement

When we bravely take steps forward we are whispering to ourselves; "This is worth it, and I won't be mastered by fear."

There's a force all of us experience when we try to do anything we should do. If you're aiming at health or impact, expect it to make an appearance. When bravery or consistency is required, it will pop up unannounced. It's real, and it's holding us all back. It's called resistance.[43]

My first move against resistance is peeling my body out of my warm bed in the darkness. I walk into the bathroom and glance at Alexa to see there's another global crisis. A few hours later, I go to Google to check on a lunch place and the headline says the economy is about to get worse. I pull up my email only to see a complaint about how we haven't sent the email yet. Then it's time for "that task" I don't want to do, so I decide to walk around and catch up with a few folks instead. I scan my texts between meetings and several people need things from me ASAP. I walk in the house, check the mailbox and get a notice of a tax mistake that will cost me thousands. When my kids don't want the dinner I made them I've had enough. I start handing out invites to my pity party. Welcome to the land of resistance. Sound familiar?

Bad news is popping up everywhere. Resistance is pressing. Criticism won't let up. Discouragement sets in thickest when we're tired. Our body, mind, heart and soul get worn down. Great leaders learn in the midst of this pressure cooker called resistance.

> If you wait until you feel like it you'll never start. Too many people quit before they ever start.

Steven Pressfield describes this perfectly in his classic *The War of Art*. "Resistance cannot be seen, touched, heard or smelled. But it can be felt. We experience it as an energy field radiating from work-in-potential. It's a repelling force. It's negative. Its aim is to shove us away, distract us, prevent us from doing our work... Resistance is not a peripheral opponent. Resistance arises from within. It is self-generated and self-perpetuated. Resistance is the enemy within."[44]

Resistance hits when we sit down to go over the spreadsheets we've been avoiding, name our quarterly goals, write the next chapter, finish the marketing campaign or schedule date nights with our spouse. If you're doing something healthy or taking new ground expect resistance. As I'm writing these words and hiding behind my laptop friends keep streaming into the coffee shop. I should've worn that 80's rocker wig.

Here's another challenge with resistance; it doesn't go away. We don't master it or graduate from it. It keeps showing up unannounced. Pressfield reminds us, "The warrior and the artist live by the same code of necessity, which dictates that the battle must be fought anew every day."[45]

The antidote to resistance is movement. The hardest part of running is getting out the door. I never quit in the first mile, but I've quit plenty of times before I put my shoes on. If you wait until you feel like it you'll never start. Too many people quit before they ever start. Author and playwright Somerset Maugham said, "I write only when inspiration strikes. Fortunately it strikes every morning at nine o'clock sharp."[46] Whether it's big or small schedule your next step and take it.

Years ago I knew our team needed to make a crucial hire, but I didn't know where to start. So I set a date on the calendar to hire the role. I had never hired this role before, and I was afraid I would hire someone with the wrong skillset. My first step was calling a friend who had been amazing in this exact role. Even though I knew she wasn't interested I hired her to help. We worked to craft the job description, put the word out and interview the qualified candidates she found. We made the perfect hire right on time. Partnering with others can get you moving faster.

Start the proposal. Make the phone call. Send the hard email. Get the gym membership. Start reading chapter one. Write the introduction. Create the job description. Put the date on the calendar (and tell your friends). Show up at the recovery group. Send the email to the coach. Turn your phone on *Do Not Disturb*. Delete the app. Delegate the task. Make the apology.

Once I start working on the project, it's easier to keep working on the project. Once I have my document open, it's easy to start writing. We're designed for movement, not stagnancy. Momentum is a game changer. Start moving and you'll feel resistance melt away. Then do it again tomorrow. And the next day. And next year.

The Obstacle: Cynicism
The Opportunity: Curiosity

Curiosity is a cold stream winding through scorching deserts of pain, anxiety and cynicism.

I sat over breakfast with Cody processing the pain he had navigated. He had picked up plenty of baggage during the almost-forced departure from his role. The pain was fresh, and I hoped some day he might seek me out for coaching when he was ready to climb his next mountain. A few years later we were, indeed, in a coaching relationship making some headway toward his future.

During one session the intensity spiked. "I'm not sure coaching can help me," he said. In a calm voice I responded, "If this isn't helpful I'm committed to ending our coaching whenever you want." I knew we could make more progress, but he had to want it. As a coach, I'm a temporary figure for months or years, scaffolding for leaders to redesign and renovate their life and leadership. I assumed it was our last session.

But Cody decided to give it one more session. I wasn't sure if he could break through the cynicism he was experiencing. I hadn't spoken to him in three weeks since our blunt session, and I was nervous. I studied the notes, and I resolved to enter our session with a posture of curiosity. I began wondering... "What was he REALLY saying about coaching not helping him? What support does he need right now? What does he want to say, but doesn't have words for? How can I show up ready to serve him boldly today without seeking to fix something or maintain the contract?"

With these questions in mind we dove straight into the deep end with scuba gear. I didn't hold back or try to salvage the coaching contract; I let him know I was with him in the depths of what he was going through. This creative, discerning, sharp leader was flooded with pain. Through tears he said, "Maybe my best days are behind me." After pausing to explore his pain and doubts, we caught some momentum. When he began a sentence with "I wonder...," I knew we'd found lift. Curiosity pushed through the surface like the first spring flower pushing through the permafrost. The last forty-five minutes were full of optimism about the future. He thanked me and said, "I'll see you soon."

When we let our pain and disappointment fester, we're in danger of becoming cynical. My brother, J.R., an author, coach and thought leader, has some helpful thoughts on cynicism. He defines cynicism as a long series of disappointments and unmet desires that generate expectations. It usually involves three feelings: hopelessness, helplessness and bitterness (which usually expresses itself as smugness). It causes us to mistrust or distrust the intentions of others.[47]

Cynicism is pervasive. Not only has cynicism soaked into our pores, it's celebrated in our culture. Leaders are particularly prone to it. Over the last decades our culture has become increasingly cynical of institutions, leaders, politics and even hope itself. Everyone looks perfect on social media. We crack jokes, send memes and distance ourselves from the issues to protect ourselves. Cynicism turns a warm heart pumping with passion into a cold heart seeking quiet escape. Anxiety and fear are hiding beneath every hardened cynical shell.

We play questions on repeat that keep us stuck.

Was I naive to think this was possible?
What are their motives?
Is it even worth the energy?
Am I/are they even capable of changing?
When are they going to turn on me?
Is it worth the risk of putting myself out there again?

How do we reverse the cynicism cycle? We take a posture of curiosity. Dr. Curt Thompson says, "The opposite of anxious is not calm; it's curious."[48] Curiosity melts cynicism like chocolate next to a flame. It says, "What if?" instead of "I could never..." It invites us to dream again, to hope again, to risk again. This invitation to cultivate curiosity has been a gift to me, and one I get to extend to my kids, my friends and my clients. If you want to lead others toward flourishing, start by practicing curiosity.

Curiosity is a discipline we must cultivate in four directions: backward, inward, forward and outward.

We can be curious looking backward. We can look back and wonder why that unfolded the way it did. It might sound like, "I wonder why that happened that way. I wonder why I/they reacted that way."

We can be curious looking inward. We can look internally and ask questions. It might sound like, "I wonder why I'm so nervous heading into this situation. I wonder what's actually going on in me. I wonder what it would look like for me to be excited walking into this room instead of afraid."

We can be curious looking forward. We can look into the near or distant future and optimistically wonder. It might sound like, "I wonder what opportunities this could lead to. What would have to be true for this situation to be energizing or life changing? How could I show up fully engaged and others-focused?"

We can be curious looking outward. We can wonder what is going on in others around us. It might sound like, "I wonder what fears or desires they have. I wonder what they are experiencing that made them react that way." (This one is particularly helpful when interacting with people who have experienced deep pain or trauma)

Cynicism keeps you stuck.
Curiosity invites you to find a crack.
Cynicism asks, "Why would it be any different this time?"
Curiosity asks, "What if things could be different?"
Cynicism brings your eyes toward the ground.
Curiosity lifts your head toward the sky.
Cynicism is a dead end.
Curiosity is an on-ramp.

Beware of curiosity killers. I see these three culprits often.

Un-named disappointments kill curiosity. When disappointments fester we can lose hope in the future. We must "name the gap" between what we hoped for and what we got.

Busyness kills curiosity. We turn inward when we're busy because we're filled to capacity. We must create space to slow down, be present and dream.

Exhaustion kills curiosity. When we're beyond tired we can only think of getting back to zero again. Seek replenishment in order to cultivate curiosity.

Practicing curiosity can look like...
Choosing to question your assumptions about your work or your field
Digging into the pain points of those you serve and dreaming about solutions
Asking, "What would have to be true in order to... ?" (name a desired result)
Reading books from other fields that could offer solutions
Revisiting a hobby just for fun
Asking great questions to a friend or coworker

Curious questions can help us dislodge cynicism. Try these.
Why did I enter this field or role?
What was I like my first week or year on the job?
What kind of actions was I taking when I believed different was possible?

PART TWO | Obstacles and opportunities along the climb

What moments shifted my thinking from what I thought was possible?
If change were possible in this area how might it come about?

Cynics aren't in the game shaping the future; they're sitting in the cheap seats telling us why it can't be done. Life and leadership can be heavy. The weight wears us down. When we get tired our defenses against cynicism weaken. In the wake of end-of-week-fatigue I often look back at my work week and wonder, "Is anyone even changing?" Ironically, it often follows an incredible week of transformation. When fatigue is high hopelessness comes knocking. When I am aware of these thoughts I know it's time to cultivate curiosity and find some margin. This is one reason practicing a sabbath is so vital. My outlook is always fresher and more buoyant on Monday.

> Cynics aren't in the game shaping the future; they're sitting in the cheap seats telling us why it can't be done.

PART THREE
Shifts to lighten the load

> *Every time you want to elevate your level of execution, performance or effectiveness, it will require a mind shift. For anything to change, the first thing that must change is your mind*[49]
> Erwin McManus

You're carrying a lot. Stop and think about everything you do each week. Caring for your family. Serving your community. Leading your team. Making a living. Meeting others expectations. That's a lot. Probably more than you think.

Our lives pick up weight as we climb. Things get added to our pack constantly. I want to extend an invitation to not only change what you're doing, but how you're doing it. Making a shift isn't the same as flipping a switch. I wish I could tell you there's a breaker switch you can flip for your life. But shifts require new ways of thinking and acting that feeldisorienting. Shifts are scary, but there is freedom on the other side of them. The exciting and the terrifying are present at the same time (I call it "terriciting.") The new and the old pull tension on us.

Shifts can be uncomfortable or downright excruciating. These valleys of pain deepen us and grow our capacity. In his masterful book *The Second Mountain*, David Brooks says, "Wealth and fame and accomplishment do not spare anybody from the valley"[50]. Others describe the ascent as a process of *orientation, disorientation,* and *reorientation*[51] or *order, disorder* and *reorder*[52]. There's a reason so many leadership and spiritual classics describe this "dark night of the soul"[53] en route to transformation. We don't like to talk about the hard, painful, and dark times in our shiny culture, but they're natural. No one is exempt.

We can't stand on summits without trudging through dusty valleys, getting caught in storms and shimmying along knife edge ridges. Shifts are paradoxes; they're heavy at first but bring lightness on the other side. Many people remain stuck where they are, because they don't know how to make a shift or aren't willing to pay the price that shifts require.

This section offers shifts leaders must make as they ascend. In this section I will help you act on them, not just learn about them. I share stories of real people with real struggles working these shifts out in real time. I've seen these shifts bring lightness and relief.

From reactive to proactive

The drift is about passivity. Life planning is about proactivity.
Michael Hyatt and Daniel Harkavy[54]

Sam is one of the most gregarious people I've ever met. He has a way of turning strangers into buddies in a moment. I met him on a high mountain experience I was hosting, and immediately connected with him. He got the invite to the mastermind experience after striking up a friendship while waiting for an Uber. That's just who Sam is.

He was living his dream of running a ranch for people to decompress from the pressures of life and return with vigor. During our coaching relationships I quickly learned he was reacting to his life, not acting upon it. Behind his brilliant ideas and marketing mind was last-minute living. I visited their incredible ranch and saw his reactivity up close. We had been working hard on naming and scheduling his priorities ahead of time so he could protect them, but new shiny things always came up. In fact, he attracted these new shiny things because he was so charismatic. He felt stuck in an unhealthy cycle.

In the middle of our coaching journey, Sam was given a second ranch. Free. Nothing. Check paid. I knew this was a life-altering gift that could position his nonprofit as a hub in his region, but it could also upend his health and his family. Sam did the hard work. He battled with his past struggles that were at the root of his dysfunction. He pulled a community around him, got serious about counseling and was completely honest with me as his coach. He began turning new corners. He turned down distracting opportunities and prioritized his family in new ways.

These ranches have become a hub for people to experience the simplicity and connection of a fire, an overnight stay, a group retreat or live music on a beautiful night. He made the shift from reactive to proactive, and is seeing the fruit every day. He is fighting for health as a dad, husband and team leader.

Getting lived by your life

So many people I meet are on life's treadmill. It's that exhausting mode where you cram new things into your calendar and just keep punching the speed dial higher to maintain what you're doing. It feels like the only option is to run harder, but you're getting more and more tired. I've been there before. It's a terrible place to live.

When we're in these seasons (or for some, decades) we aren't living our life; we're getting lived by it. In this mode our days and weeks plan us, we don't plan them. Our schedule drags us through the week. We regret committing to so many things, but it's all too overwhelming to cancel. We schedule later into the evening, skip another lunch, set the alarm an hour earlier and convince ourselves we'll get to the gym next week. We pretend everything is fine, and convince ourselves that we'll slow down soon. I believe some people move across the country, because it's the only way they know to jump off life's treadmill and start over.

But here's the problem. Overwhelm is pre-burnout. In this mode we're tired, task-driven, and bent toward bad decisions. Ironically, in our state of overwhelm we are convinced we cannot afford time for rest and recovery, the very things we need to replenish. This is one path to the burnout spiral.

We don't make wise decisions when we're living reactive for several reasons.

PART THREE | Shifts to lighten the load

We see only the problems, not our priorities.
We see only short-term fixes, not long-term investments.
We're in a frenzied state. Our body and mind are on overdrive.
We get tunnel vision, seeing only the task and looking past the people.
We're trying to catch up, not get ahead.
We miss things, get sloppy and shed good habits.
We suck others into the same frenzy of reactivity.

We cannot design our lives when we are reacting to them. Sometimes we must react, but taking up residence in the land of reactivity will create chaos for us and those around us. We've all functioned here occasionally, but we cannot live in this "fight or flight" reality for long without neglecting priorities and hurting those we love, ourselves or both.

> Proactivity allows a leader to play defense and offense, protecting their priorities while capitalizing on new opportunities.

We must instead learn to live and lead proactively. In this mode we zoom out, look ahead, and make intentional decisions. When we live and lead proactively we have agency inside of our life. We can evaluate the opportunities and structure for health. Proactive living allows us to do the following.

Make decisions based on priorities, not problems.
Slow down to examine the tradeoffs and possibilities of saying yes.
Be present with people, not just see a list of tasks.
Get creative, working around obstacles without being defeated by them.
Experience the momentum of being ahead.
Add new things to life and work without toppling other things.
Show up fully and bring our best.
Work from rest, not just rest from work.
Cultivate proactive, healthy culture around us.

Proactivity allows a leader to play defense and offense, protecting their priorities while capitalizing on new opportunities. Proactive leaders know what matters to them and can evaluate anything new through that lens. This proactive mindset allows a leader to slow down, get the necessary information, examine the commitment and decide whether it moves them toward or away from where they want to be. When we live and lead proactively, we offer that same posture as a gift to those around us.

> **Reflect on this shift**
>
> In which areas of my life or leadership am I living reactively?
>
> How is that impacting me and others around me?
>
> What steps can I take to move toward proactivity?

From confusion to clarity

It's okay to be stressed, but it's not okay to be confused.
Mike Bone, Filmmaker

When I met Steve he was a mid-level executive with low-level confidence. Despite being a former college athlete, and having served in several meaningful business roles, his self-confidence was low. He shared about his friends who were amazing leaders, but failed to see it in himself.

His boss connected him to me for coaching in hopes it could raise his capacity. A few sessions into coaching it was clear to me that Steve didn't understand his role. Confusion rolled downhill from the top of the organization. If he was going to thrive in his role he must work to gain clarity.

He accepted the challenge. His hunger propelled him. Every session, he shared the progress he made and the areas he wanted to make progress on. He implemented development programs for the staff, analyzed sales channels, designed and implemented a new review process, and identified areas the company could maximize impact and income. Steve was raising the water level.

During one session the fruit of his work became tangible. He was ready to seek greater responsibility and compensation. He had done the hard work to gain internal clarity and taken courageous steps which had translated to external impact. I saw something new blooming in Steve; confidence. I'm not talking about some kind of "fake it 'til you make it" bravado or "close your eyes and believe it's going to happen" flavor of confidence. There is an unmistakeable grounded confidence that comes from knowing you can bring value.

I've experienced this shift myself. Early in my coaching and consulting work I was nervous walking into team trainings or group sessions. This is the moment you realize you have pit stains and won't be lifting your arms up as you present. Why was I so nervous? I was focused on myself, not how I could serve the group. Instead of investing my energy into studying the team and looking for cracks to multiply value, I was focused on my performance. It's hard to serve others deeply when you're focused on yourself.

After years of clarifying my processes and watching them impact leaders and teams I walk into team sessions expectant and confident. I can't wait to experience moments of transformation. I've seen the principles and tools help leaders and teams get healthy and reach greater impact. Clarity develops confidence.

Remember, clarity is not the same as certainty. Certainty is absolute. The dictionary definition is "an assured fact."[55] We actually cannot gain certainty. We don't know where the world is heading, what events will unfold for our family, how the economy will behave or how innovations will shape our work. Gripping for certainty only leads to overwhelm and anxiety, and is bound to crumble anyway.

Certainty is an allusion, but clarity is attainable. The dictionary definition of clarity is "freedom from ambiguity."[56] Where certainty clings for absolute assurance, clarity seeks to eliminate ambiguity. Proactively seeking clarity can help us take the right steps. Gaining clarity is not only possible; it's essential to leadership. A leader has a responsibility to fight for clarity. A team or organization will never be more clear than the leader.

Internal clarity shapes external actions

Most decisions leaders face are not between good and bad but between good and best. When we were young, we looked for good opportunities, but as we mature we must look for the best opportunities. Good opportunities can become the major distraction for leaders. When life is unfolding quickly it can be hard to decipher good opportunities from the best ones. This is why we must clarify what matters ahead of time.

Philosopher Miroslav Volf asks the arresting question, "What is worth wanting?"[57] What is it for you? More money? More time with family? More leisure? More responsibility? More friendships? More opportunities? If we do not know what we truly want we will live confused and unfulfilled. Desire and action are a two way street; our desires shape our actions and our actions shape our desires. We all have to ask the clarifying question, "What's worth fighting for?" If we're fighting for everything we're fighting for nothing.

> We all have to ask the clarifying question, "What's worth fighting for?" If we're fighting for everything we're fighting for nothing.

A few years ago I came to a painful realization that I was fighting for someone else's dream, not mine. Instead of letting others influence me I had let them change me. It required me simplifying several areas of my life. I had to descend into the valley before I could ascend my next peak. My ego was on life support. That clarity was painful and disorienting, but led me to experiencing a new kind of freedom to be uniquely me.

> **Reflect on this shift**
>
> Which area of my life feels foggy right now?
>
> How will I clarify realities and steps forward in that area?
>
> What is worth fighting for in my life and leadership?

From triage to priorities

How we spend our days is, of course, how we spend our lives
Annie Dillard

Bethany is one of the most energetic people I've ever met. Her contagious personality lights up a room and inspires teams. When she invited me to coach her, the first thing I noticed was her speed. She moved lightning fast through emails, strategy and hiring. Sometimes she had to go back and undo hasty decisions or apologize for assuming things without the full story. This impulse for speed had helped advance her career, but it was holding her back from making wise decisions.

In our coaching sessions we worked on slowing down to clarify her priorities and design processes to protect them. The quality of her decisions and her leadership capacity increased. She showed up early to our sessions clear on what she wanted to discuss. She learned to ask questions before coming to conclusions. Her presence changed from chaotic to calm. Bethany made a shift from triage to priorities.

In triage mode we're thinking about survival, not priorities. We're busy, but not very effective. Perhaps the worst part is that triage mode is contagious to our teams. We whip them into a frenzy, and they believe crazy is normal. In our rush we forget about the people right in front us and the things that deeply matter to us. We scan our email between meetings, responding to anything that smells like an emergency while neglecting the things that make us effective and move the organization down the field.

What will kill them first?

I went through a nine day training course in Wilderness First Responder. We learned how to help those injured in the wilderness get to safety. For our final exam half the class were actors and the other half of us had to work together to assess and safely transport victims from a major accident. As the sun was going down, we walked upon a staged plane crash. The victims were screaming and writhing in pain covered with makeup and fake blood from gnarly injuries.

For the previous nine days we were trained to ask, "What will kill them first?" We would treat the most serious injuries first to preserve lives. We learned to walk past someone screaming at the top of their lungs from a broken ankle to treat someone silently suffering from a punctured lung. Our instructors evaluated how we assessed and treated life threatening injuries while avoiding minor ones. Many of the screamers were left painfully unattended for the next few hours (sorry guys but, your ankle is going to heal).

This mindset works when you're coming up on a plane crash, but doesn't work very well when you're leading. Leaders who live rushed are bound to fall into this triage mindset asking, "What will kill us first?" Without a plan and the calmness to execute the plan human nature takes over. The brain stays in high alert, and we make bad decisions, losing sight of what matters most to us or the organization. Once you're leading at a certain level there is always one more thing to take care of; the screamers are everywhere.

A leader living from priorities is asking, "What matters most right now?" They've formulated a plan based on priorities, and they follow the plan. Will emergencies arise occasionally? Absolutely. If we don't define emergencies ahead of time everything feels like an emergency in the moment. Sometimes I have six minutes left at the end of the day and ten emails I'd like to get to. My brain tells me, "You HAVE to get these answered before you get in your car!" My brain is telling me

PART THREE | Shifts to lighten the load

there's a plane crash, but in reality the emails can wait until tomorrow. They aren't worth being late to pick up daughter. I glance at my *Right Side up Journal* seeing I have gotten everything done for the day I had committed to. I take a deep breath, close my laptop, and hop in my car to go meet my precious daughter.

Think about all the things screaming for equal attention from us.

Emails and texts. Communication outlets are out of control. We must develop a system for answering these that dignifies people without controlling us.

Finances. Budget deficits or sudden financial changes can throw off our whole day or dominate meetings.

Those we love. Our families will be at our death beds, and our employees won't. It's easy to come home late or jump back in the inbox after dinner to put out one more fire.

Rest. We need rest if we are going to work effectively and stay healthy. This must be a priority to leaders or we will not be able to lead well for the long haul. Our creativity, passion for our work and mental sharpness will go flat unless we prioritize rest.

> **Reflect on this shift**
>
> Which area/s of my life or leadership are in triage mode?
>
> What are my top three priorities in this season?
>
> What actions will I take to protect them?

From time management to energy investment

Where you invest your love you invest your life.
Mumford and Sons

I love creating spaces where leaders can be themselves — no bull#*&%, no pretending, no need to impress. On one particular day the table was filled with business owners. Every leader was feeling the end-of-year-squeeze approaching. The assumption was, "If we could just create more time our stress would decrease and impact would increase." While I was glad we'd curated a vulnerable space, I didn't agree with their assessment. They didn't need more time. They needed to shift their thinking. They actually needed more energy.

So many tools in leadership focus on managing our time. This makes sense. Time is precious. We can do meaningful things with it, and it's easy to measure. We measure work weeks, meetings and vacations in hours and days. But if we were somehow given all the time in the world and didn't know what it was for it wouldn't help us. If you don't know the most important actions to focus on you drift toward ineffectiveness and exhaustion. The currency of leadership is energy, not time.

The currency of leadership is energy, not time.

Physics describes the difference between potential energy and kinetic energy. Potential movement is very different from actual movement. It's more important for us to invest our energy wisely than to spend our time wisely. I know that may sound strange, but I promise you it's a helpful shift that can help you bypass burnout and lead for the long haul.

If you desire to impact more people, you'll need to learn to multiply your time and your energy. You only have so much time, but you can learn to utilize energy to your advantage. When we understand how to invest our energy in the right places, combustion happens, transformation unfolds, and fulfillment skyrockets. Minutes of doing the best things can trump days or weeks of doing good things. Ten minutes of looking my kids in the eyes hearing about their day is far better than five hours of being in the next room on my laptop. Ten minutes in the morning mapping out my day in my *Right Side up Journal* gives me a plan to follow for the next twelve hours. An hour of creating the right plan can diffuse a quarter of misalignment on the team.

Think R.O.E. — return on energy

When we move from spending to investing we make a fundamental shift. Spenders work for money, but investors make their money work for them. Investing energy works the same way. The leaders who invest their energy know when and where their energy brings the best returns. This is why I love leading *The Six Types of Working Genius* trainings with teams.[58] This tool helps leaders and teams understand the best areas to invest their energy for great returns. Other tools like *The Birkman Method* and *Clifton Strengths* can be helpful as well.

Financial investors focus on R.O.I. (return on investment), but leaders must focus on R.O.E. (return on energy). Content creation and tool development have a high R.O.E. for me. I invested precious energy into writing this book, and people across the world can be nourished by it for a fraction of the cost of coaching. My team and I invest energy in developing tools that help leaders long after their coaching journey is finished. Some leaders focus their best energy on inspiring teams through delivering keynotes, others focus on leading incredible executive meetings and others on recruiting and developing young talent. Clarifying your R.O.E. can help you multiply your energy for years to come.

The most effective leaders develop rhythms to invest regularly in their growth, their family, and their replenishment. They work with the grain of their energy, not against it. The Annual Energy Map tool helps leaders look proactively at what's coming. This tools allows leaders across industries to evaluate personal, family and work needs ahead of time.

This tool can also help you prepare your mind, heart, schedule, team and family for the realities that are on the way. During a coaching session a leader may acknowledge they are in a challenging two month sprint, but they can visually see the light at the end of the tunnel. This has become a great tool to unifying marriages and teams around the unique needs of a season.

> **Reflect on this shift**
>
> How could the shift from managing my time to investing my energy be freeing?
>
> What three activities give me the highest R.O.E. (return on energy)?

Invest some time on the opposite page filling out the Annual Energy Map for the next year, or at least the next quarter.

STAY FORTH DESIGNS: ANNUAL ENERGY MAP

NAME _____

20__

ENERGY REQUIRED	BIG EVENTS	BREAKS I WILL TAKE	CHALLENGES	FEARS
JAN __/10				
FEB __/10				
MARCH __/10				
APRIL __/10				
MAY __/10				
JUNE __/10				
JULY __/10				
AUG __/10				
SEPT __/10				
OCT __/10				
NOV __/10				
DEC __/10				

Which month will require the most energy: in my job? _____ in my family? _____ in my relationships? _____ personally? _____

Which month will be my busiest month? _____ Why? _____

© Stay Forth Designs | Find more helpful tools at StayForth.com/resources

From intuitive to intentional

*Linear results create a one-time benefit,
residual results reap benefits again and again*
Greg McKeown[59]

B rad is one of those guys you just want to be across the table from. He drives a few hours to buy a burger for a friend who's struggling. He's also a great leader. After coaching Brad for a few months, some stress fractures rose to the surface of his leadership. He was pulled in many different directions outside of his organization. People were asking him to speak to groups, strategize processes, serve on boards, and inspire groups of leaders. He knew these cracks had the potential to derail his leadership.

These opportunities were all *good*, but were they *best*? During our coaching sessions he worked to clarify the difference between the best opportunities and the good ones based on his unique design, family needs, and leadership season.

Like many founders, Brad held the keys to organizational knowledge. When a decision needed to be made, he made it quickly and intuitively. He had over-relied on his sharp intuition. When these decisions came up, all eyes in the room shifted to him. This works for a young or small organization, but it stops working as an organization gets larger and matures. Brad needed to make a major shift from intuitive decision-making to intentional decision making. Over the next few years he fought to clarify the best opportunities and spread the decision-making power throughout the organization. He even received a long sabbatical that would stress-test these intentional systems.

> People need to know what matters to an organization and develop a process for making wise decisions in light of those priorities.

I've walked through this same shift with dozens of leaders. Relying on the intuition of a leader to make every decision stops working at some point in the life of the organization. It accidentally generates disempowerment and confusion for the team and decision fatigue for the leader. The leader must help the team discover intentional processes to follow without relying on them. People need to know what matters to an organization and develop a process for making wise decisions in light of those priorities. This shift requires moving the focus from the decisions that need to be made to the values behind the decisions. This shift never happens on accident.

The barriers to this shift

It's all they know. Many leaders who start an organization haven't experienced the realities of a growing organization. Getting perspective from outside the organization is vital when you hit this inflection point. It's hard to see the forest when you're stuck in the underbrush.

It requires slowing down. Ironically, it requires slowing down in order to speed up. Pulling in the team, and perhaps an outside coach or consultant to create processes, can unlock a breakthrough. It requires an investment up front, but it can pay off big in the future.

It requires intentionally giving up control. People naturally look to the founder or leader to make decisions. They must make the move to voluntarily give up control and empower others to make decisions

PART THREE | Shifts to lighten the load

and shape processes. Ironically, they often want to be free from these decisions and responsibilities, but they don't know how.

The benefits of this shift

It leads to effectiveness. Intentional processes don't guarantee growth, but they pave a pathway for it. The leader often realizes they were a bottleneck to growth or they were driving growth at an unrealistic pace. With some work the team is able to make wiser decisions that pull the weight off the leader or leadership team.

It allows deeper team engagement. When decisions move from the brain of one leader to the collective brain of a team they can make better decisions. They also share the weight of the decisions and the work. Engagement and ownership grow at multiple levels.

It creates space for the leader to pursue new opportunities. A founder or leader is often ready for a side challenge. One founder of a large company missed the product development and innovation side of the business. He gave more responsibility to the rest of the executive team, and reinvested much of his week into product innovation. His fulfillment levels rose, and they began innovating again. Another founder wanted to coach leaders across the country without leaving the helm of the organization, so he invited his team to help shape leaders across the country with him. A leaders' ability to pursue side projects without hurting the organization is directly linked to how much they have intentionally equipped the team to carry the weight.

When a leader moves from intuitive to intentional others feel empowered to lead, and the leader has space redirect their energy.

> **Reflect on this shift**
>
> What processes or decisions do I need to shift from intuitive to intentional?
>
> How might this benefit my team or my organization?
>
> If I had more space in my schedule how would I reinvest it?

From doer to developer

Once you assume a leadership role, your job performance is no longer measured by your personal accomplishments. Instead, your job is to unleash the creative potential in others.
Todd Henry[60]

Sarah was at the top of her project management field. She had honed and refined her work by helping some of the best organizations in her field run smoothly while changing the world. But, like many founders who make "the jump", she wanted to shape organizations at a deeper level. She launched her own company with a fire to be an excellent, dignifying business while helping organizations live out their mission. It was a joy to help her actualize that vision.

During a group coaching program, she shared vulnerably about not knowing how to move from a technical worker to a CEO. She always listened well, gave helpful feedback, and clarified her next step for the business. She identified and empowered a younger leader to shape the company alongside her. She and her teammate, Kristen, expanded and equipped a team, constantly replacing themselves. Coaching sessions with Sarah and Kristen were focused and collaborative. The organization continues to take new ground and break their perceived barriers. They made the shift many leaders struggle to make; from doer to developer.

The transition from doer to developer happens with careful intentionality over a period of time. Leaders may have to retain some technical aspects, but constantly seek to replace themselves while increasing the capacity of the team. Here are a few key distinctions between these two.

Doers execute the technical work in an organization.
Developers cultivate the team to execute the work.
Doers work on raising their capacity.
Developers work on raising the capacity of the team.
Doers prepare themselves for new tasks.
Developers equip a team to break through new levels.

> Developing others requires transferring what's in the head of the leader into the processes of the team.

In his book *The Emyth* Michael Gerber unpacks three archetypes; the technician, the manager and the entrepreneur. "The technician lives in the present and is focused on doing the work of making it, selling it and delivering it. The manager focuses on achieving results through people and systems, focusing on the present and strategizing for the future. The entrepreneur defines the business and focuses on closing the gap between where the business is today and where they want it to be."[61] A founder has all three of these personalities inside them, and they are in constant tension. The technician, or doer, prefers to work *in the business* instead of *on the business*, so they can have a limited viewpoint and get buried in the work.[62]

The shift from doer to developer requires new thinking and new skills that help develop others to carry out the work. Developing others requires transferring what's in the head of the leader into the processes of the team. This is another paradox that requires more energy in the present but gives back more energy in the future.

In order to make this shift a leader has to lay down their ego. The best leaders accomplish tasks through teams. The individual contributor is valuable to the mission, but the one who can develop teams is invaluable. Tom Rath, Carry Conchie and the team at Gallup did research and found the most effective leaders do these four things: "The most effective leaders are always investing in strengths, surround themselves with the right people, then maximize their team and understand their followers needs.[63] In short; they develop themselves and develop others. They are not just geniuses, they are genius makers.

We often think about a team only for technical support. I've found leaders tend to over-estimate their need for the technical support, and under-estimate their need for relational and moral support. I encourage leaders to pull a life team around them. A life team supports leaders in the cracks and gaps of their life and leadership. Wise leaders build teams around them who help them to keep leading at a high level. I'm grateful for two other family men with deep integrity who ask me challenging questions about my life and leadership. Who encourages you when you're doubting yourself and your work? Who helps you process big decisions? Who prays for you when you're down? Who inspires you when you're creatively flat?

As an author and coach, I love helping people clarify their messages and turn them into books. The process of writing a book is notorious for wearing leaders down. If you're writing a book you'll need technical help from an editor and a designer, but you'll also need an encourager to check in with you when you doubt if your message even matters. You may even need other writers to ask you where you're stalled or if you're hitting your deadlines.

If you want your team and organization to mature, you must mature. The greatest impact you can make is raising others up and increasing their capacity. Not only does this make leadership lighter for you; it engages and empowers others.

Reflect on this shift

In what areas am I holding too much responsibility? What beliefs are informing this?

Who can I develop into greatness?

What tasks and areas will I invite them into?

From efficient to effective

Be efficient with things and effective with people
Stephen M.R. Covey

"I have to be honest with you about our last meeting." I braced for what he was about to say. "During that lunch I felt like I was just one more thing on your list. I don't want to meet again if it feels like that."

The words stung. I vividly remember sliding the lunch into a ninety minute block between clients; rushing there, rushing to reconnect with him, rushing to take the check and rushing back to my office. He was exactly right. I had treated him like one more task.

During a season of my leadership, I took on too much, and I lost focus. I believed the lie that people were one more task to mark off the list. I rushed interactions with coaching clients and friends. When we lose focus we rush, and when we rush we treat other humans like machines. True leadership is about developing the people who get the tasks done; it's more about effectiveness than efficiency.

Peter Drucker, father of organizational leadership and mentor to Jim Collins, defines effectiveness as "Doing the right things well."[64] His definition begs us to ask two questions:

What are the right things for me to be doing?
How can I do them well?

The simplicity of these questions is helpful as we cut through the wilderness climbing our peak. You can't and shouldn't do it all. Slowing down now to clarify the right things and how we do them well will always come back to help us later.

> When we don't know what to do we settle for doing anything. Activity is not the same as action.

When we don't know what to do we settle for doing anything. Activity is not the same as action. When we're in task mode we can shift to an efficiency mindset with people and accidentally treat them like machines. Effectiveness and efficiency are very different. Focusing on effectiveness can lead us to do the right things well. Focusing on efficiency can lead us to do all the things well enough.

Efficiency mindset isn't always bad. I'm in efficiency mode when I make a quick trip to the grocery store, knock off Sunday afternoon chores or prepare to leave on a big trip. Is there a time for both? Of course. I like Covey's grid of focusing on effectiveness with people and efficiency with things[65]. The challenge is we have to both get tasks done and develop people to get tasks done.

Healthy leaders live in effectiveness mindset, but can become efficient when needed. If you lead people at any level, they are your greatest asset to steward, equip, and care for. Like my lunch companion, they will feel it when we rush and treat them like they're just a cog in a wheel.

But when we slow down to meet their needs we can push the mission forward more effectively. Choosing effectiveness builds a healthy culture, reminds people they matter, and retains employees. I watched the pandemic gut organizations who viewed employees with efficiency mindset. Their best talent left and went somewhere that showed them value and meaning.

Efficiency mindset is driving our culture, and it's easy to slip into. We live in a culture of excess. Marketers, companies, pop-up ads and our own brains whisper to us, "More IS more. Do more. Buy more. Be more. Consume more. Then you will happy, fulfilled, successful and content." We've become a culture who hoards memories, goods, services, experiences, stuff, and ideas, and we wonder why meaning has plummeted and anxiety has skyrocketed.

The path to fulfillment in this culture of excess is through elimination. We must clarify what REALLY matters to us, and shed the rest. This is why comparison that leads to envy is so dangerous. The good life to someone else is your nightmare. Your best day is their worst day. Their dream job would feel like a cage to you. Their idea of a great vacation is the opposite of what you and your family would love.

If we aim at efficiency, we will eventually drive others and ourselves even harder for results. This is the recipe for burnout and an unhealthy work culture. This mentality of treating people like machines is called "depersonalization" and is a significant contributor to burnout.[66] We depersonalize, or dehumanize, ourselves, and others pretending we are machines that need only a drop of oil instead of love, care, encouragement, and rest. When we act limitless, we will eventually trip over our limits. When we deprive ourselves of rest and margin we will, indeed, discover we are not a machine.

What makes the struggle worse is we celebrate efficiency. We reward people for getting things done quickly and cheer on high-producers with the 'compliment', "She's a machine!" Really? Is that what we want?

The roots of an effective leader

An effective leader develops qualities below the surface, then eventually bears fruit above the surface. Let's get more specific on how I define an effective leader. An effective leader *comprehends their influence, lives healthy, practices self-awareness, works with the grain of their gifting,* and *moves at a sustainable pace.* Let's break these down.

Comprehends their influence. They understand the impact they have on others and their potential to model health or dysfunction.

Lives healthy. They are integrated in their heart, soul, mind, body and relationships. They have clarified their values and needs, and they prioritize these things.

Practices self-awareness. They can regularly identify their emotions, their assets and their liabilities.

Works with the grain of their gifting. They understand their unique design and have the ability to maximize their talents.

Moves at a sustainable pace. They progress at a level of speed and energy that can be mirrored by their team and be sustained over multiple seasons.

Do a quick assessment giving yourself a 1-10 on each of these.

How well do I comprehend my influence on others?
How healthy do I believe I am?
How self-aware do I believe I am?
How well am I working with the grain of my gifting?
How sustainable is my pace?

Now get three or four people who are close to you in different areas of your life to assess you in this same areas.

The fruits of an effective leader
When the roots are cultivated the fruit begins to bud. Did you know it takes most fruit trees a few years to begin producing edible fruit and a few more years before the tree produces fully? With patient practice healthy roots produce healthy fruit. When you steward the things in your influence today you'll be given more opportunities in the future.

The internal fruit of effectiveness is fulfillment. It's satisfying to grow. It makes us feel alive. Our shoulders rise and so does our self-respect. When we're leading effectively it's easy to fall in love with the process, instead of the result. Our craft and our skills grow. We begin to see we're doing something that matters deeply and is worth investing in. It doesn't mean our work is perfect or easy. Investing time and energy into something that matters is meaningful, and compels us to do our best day after day even when we must suffer for it.

The external fruit of effectiveness is impact. It's also satisfying when we see how our work impact others. This can't be the only reason why we keep doing our work, but it sure is helpful to get these indicators occasionally. At times we will hear others growth, joy, or gratitude.

When things grow quickly sometimes it produces issues. Organizations that grow too quickly often have to clean up messes later. When leaders gain visibility or a following quickly they skip the season of hidden growth. This obscurity can be a gift — a time to focus on cultivating the roots, developing their character and growing their skills. If you're not seeing an impact right now keep nourishing the roots below the soil.

> **Reflect on this shift**
>
> Which area/s of my leadership need to shift from efficiency to effectiveness?
>
> Which area could use more attention; my influence, health, self-awareness, gifting or pace?

7 Shifts to lighten the load

1. From reactive to proactive

2. From confusion to clarity

3. From triage to priorities

4. From time management to energy investment

5. From intuitive to intentional

6. From doer to developer

7. From efficient to effective

#AntiBurnout Book

PART FOUR
Habits to keep you climbing

Launching something takes a burst of energy, but sustaining takes intention and discipline. We must cultivate habits to stay healthy and grounded if we desire to go the distance in our leadership. Sustainable change is the pathway up the gulleys and ridges of the leadership climb. This section outlines habits great leaders do repeatedly that separate them from the rest.

Learn like your life depends on it (because it does)

The illiterate of the 21st century will not be those who cannot read and write, but those who cannot learn, unlearn, and relearn.
Alvin Toffler

If you want to shape the future become a learner. Ask questions. Get curious. Listen to what others are learning. Stay sharp. But this doesn't mean you need to always be reading a stack of books. I used to say "leaders are readers" until I realized how many leaders learn in others ways. Over the years I've discovered a surprising amount of leaders wrestle with ADHD or dyslexia, and have struggled to read their whole lives. I've amended the phrase to "leaders are learners". Some hungry learners struggle with reading and think, "well, I must not be a leader". Hogwash. Reading is just one way to learn.

One leader I was coaching was worn down by the constant pressure to read more. At the same time he had access to three of the best sages in the country who he talked with regularly. He was exhausted from information overload and full of shame for not reading enough. I told him to stop reading for a while. About six months later he was reading voraciously again and loving it.

We have to think differently about how we learn. Leaders in the trenches are naturally learning so much every week that they might be better served to journal, reflect on their experiential learning or converse with others leaders in their industry. How you learn should sprout from how your brain is wired. We've never had more options for how to learn. Mentors can help us shortcut decades of mistakes. Coaching can elevate our habits and execution to new levels. Masterclasses, podcasts, mastermind groups, wisdom circles, webinars and TED talks can quickly distill hard-fought wisdom.

> We have this bad habit in the West of learning more about what we should do instead of actually doing it.

A hungry leader asked me to coach him as he launched his coaching business. He had been highly successful in the tech industry, and found deep fulfillment mentoring others in his field. During one of our sessions he asked for book recommendations, and I only sent him one. He texted me the next day saying he had finished it and was ready for the next book. I told him there are no more books to read right now, but I wanted to hear his action steps from the one he read. At the end of our next session he had distilled four big takeaways from the book and created his plan of action.

We have this bad habit in the West of learning more about what we should do instead of actually doing it. This habit is called "procrastination through education". Sometimes the focus on reading convinces us to keep reading books instead of taking steps. We grew up being told what to learn, but few of us ever learned how to learn.

For most of humanity except the recent past we've learned through the apprentice model. Many fields still prepare leaders for their work in this way.

APPRENTICE MODEL

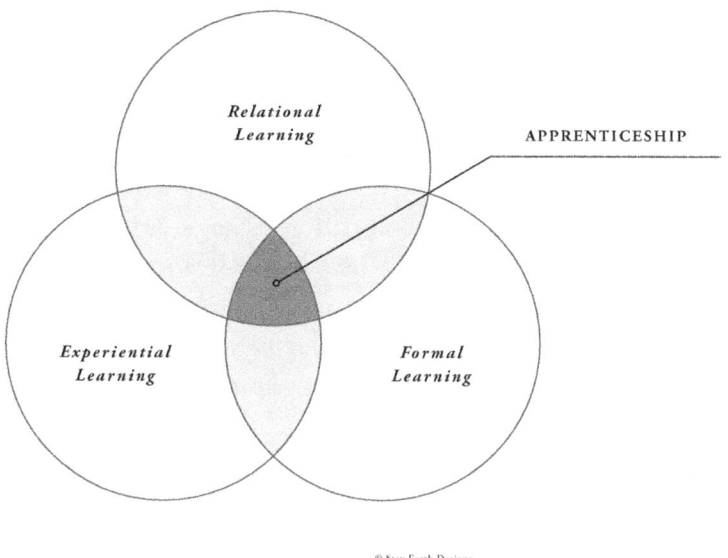

© Stay Forth Designs

We need to return to learning more in these ways. I bet one of the following is strong for you, and one could really use some attention. Many times one circle has gotten too large while others have been neglected. Leaders can even craft development plans for themselves by using these three areas.

Relational learning. This is where we learn from others. They share the victories, failures and the secrets behind their work. Others can shortcut your time to success and help you avoid a lot of pain. Make it a habit to learn from great people. Truth be told, this is one reason I host a podcast; I want to have conversations with world-class leaders.

Experiential learning. This is where we learn by doing. Aristotle commented, "It is by doing just acts that a just man is produced"[67] Learning crystalizes during our experiences. We have largely neglected this in the West, and people are hungry for experiences where they can learn through immersion.

Formal learning. This is where we learn through written, auditory and visual methods. Many leaders soak in new ideas as they walk their dog, do the dishes, work out, and commute. It's easy to learn from experts on YouTube and TED stages. Formal learning is necessary, but it's easier and cheaper to get than ever before. We need to focus on applying our formal learning instead of just reading or hearing it. Formal learning is not bad, it's just incomplete.

A few years ago I was disappointed by the cohorts we were leading. People weren't returning a year later with new patterns of life that were leading to freedom and culture change. Despite my coaching posture all week in the experiential and relational learning zones I focused on formal learning. I dumped information on attendees week after week. These were helpful principles, but I knew the format had to change. So I gave myself a yellow card, ran off the field and rehatched a new strategy.

I shifted from teaching new ideas to helping people practice new skills. I extended the length of each session to avoid rush and maximize discussion time. I limited the teaching time (yes, it's hard for every communicator), and paired every skill with at least one tool they would practice that week. I even hosted a live coaching segment at the end of each session for the brave ones. People turned from observers to participants. My fulfillment rose, and so did their growth. The next time through the cohort I added a peer coaching dynamic where they learned to coach each other through their obstacles instead of just watching me do it. Every leader can add depth to their leadership or communication by focusing on these aspects of the apprentice model.

People of action will shape the future and fail along the way. Whether you're cheering him on or scowling at him Elon Must just keeps activating on his seemingly crazy ideas. Battery powered self driving cars - ridiculous! When I launched Stay Forth I felt completely under-prepared to help leaders increase their health and impact, but I knew I needed to jump. I made plenty of mistakes, especially in the first year. I look back and laugh at some of the risks we took. I hit plenty of moments where I wondered if I had what it took to help leaders make massive shifts. I've never regretted the decision to invest in the health of leaders full-time, but I have plenty of blisters from the climb. It has forced me to learn like my life depends on it.

What calling has compelled you so deeply you're willing to suffer for it? For me, it's helping leaders get healthy and create healthy cultures around them. What is this for you? If you just can't shake a thought or a desire, you may have to pay more attention to it. I could not stop thinking about how we train leaders to launch, but not to sustain. Leaders are the catalysts shaping cultures. When they get healthy, others around them get healthy. When they grow, others grow. When their companies expand, others get jobs and provide for their families. When they create dignified workplaces, people go home fulfilled. I'll give my life to that, and fail if needed!

A close friend of mine became the mayor of our city. He was an unorthodox candidate in many ways and a "first" in many categories. His first act when he took office was to create a listening tour. For his first one hundred days, he and his team created listening spaces all over our city to understand the true issues people were facing. The higher you ascend in your leadership role, the more important listening becomes. Learners are shaped and formed as they shape and form others. Listening and learning keeps us close to the action. The future of our communities, businesses and nonprofits depend on the quality of our learning.

God has wired every person to have an impact on those around them. Brilliance is no guarantee you'll shape the future; I'll bet on the hungry ones who keep taking the steps everyone else was too scared to take.

> **Reflect on your learning**
>
> What lies have I believed about learning?
>
> Which aspect of my learning needs more attention; relational, experiential or formal?
>
> Who am I listening to and learning from on a regular basis?

Seize little slivers of opportunity

You can't connect the dots looking forward;
you can only connect them looking backwards
Steve Jobs

I opened my inbox to see an opportunity to give a main stage talk at a conference in my city. As I read further it was clear they were giving me the "hometown treatment", where people don't pay you because you don't have to fly to the event you're speaking at. It felt like a slap in the face to me and my craft when I knew the other speakers would be getting paid.

I waited for a few days with a rotten attitude to respond to the email. I considered turning it down just to make a point (picture a kid in the corner pouting with his arms crossed). My coaching schedule was busy, and I wasn't sure it was worth it. Once I moved past my grumpiness I wondered, "How could this be an opportunity?" I had home court advantage in my city, and I could connect leaders in unique ways.

Unsure of exactly how I would do this I responded yes to the speaking opportunity. I began making plans to create a dinner experience that would connect leaders to one another and be inspired by what was unfolding in my city. I reserved a restaurant, looked over the speaker list and began making invites. A few days later the event organizers invited me to a speaker dinner the night before the dinner I was already planning. Four days earlier I was considering turning down the opportunity to speak, now I had two dinners booked with fascinating people two nights in a row.

> We all get moments where opportunity finds us. They require imagination, because they're often disguised as obstacles or disappointments.

Both of these dinners unfolded beautifully, exposing me to new people and new ideas. One leader realized they didn't have a hotel booked while he walked out of the restaurant, and he crashed on our couch that night. He has become a friend and introduced me to countless leaders and several great opportunities. These two dinners created relationships and opportunities that have led to new friendships, over a dozen coaching clients, invitations to other events and countless opportunities to serve leaders.

We all get moments where opportunity finds us. They require imagination, because they're often disguised as obstacles or disappointments. Most people aren't prepared for them, many people won't see them, few will seize them. If we change our mindset to look for opportunities they can become open doors. I'm in awe of the opportunities I've gotten. Some days I feel like I'm living someone else's life. When I look backward my life is full of doors that have opened to me. Here are some slivers that grew into something greater.

A conversation in line at an event turned into one of my biggest coaching contracts.

A $25 lunch led to an organizational partnership that yielded multiple overseas trips, two fly-in fishing trips and several other events.

A dinner conversation inspired my daughter and I to change previous travel plans and explore Europe.

A comment in line at a coffee shop turned into an opportunity to work in Antarctica and travel the world.

A breakfast to reconnect with a friend turned into a book contract.

An email inquiring about empty space grew into into a coworking space. A few conversations for advice led to co-owning a property in the mountains.

A mistaken identity led to a wilderness trip and a long-term friendship (I literally thought the dude was someone else then invited him on a trip).

A request to fill in for a friend while he went on vacation led to my first conversation with my wife, Julie.

Seize the little sliver you're given and it may lead to more. Has it worked every time? Of course not. I've been ghosted plenty of times, saw potential that never amounted to anything, and tried stuff that felt like a waste of time. But every risk I've taken has bolstered my courage and helped me grow. One time I was getting mixed messages from a very busy leader trying to nail down their coaching contract. I needed to know if they were in or out so I could plan my coaching schedule for the next year. I booked a flight to meet him at his second home before even asking permission (I don't necessarily recommend this, but it was the right call in that moment). We had only a two hour block to connect before I turned around and caught my plane. He eventually passed on coaching, but thanked me for my support and paid me for my time. We're still friends today.

While you may not get advanced notice you can prepare to seize these moments. Have your pitch ready to share at any moment. Know your ideal client so well that you can recognize them in a split second. When someone says, "We should set up a meeting," go ahead and set up a time. When people tell you they're interested, follow up with an email. Big moments will find you disguised in many different outfits. Make sure not to turn them down too quickly.

> **Reflect on slivers of opportunity**
> Describe a moment that unlocked a surprising opportunity...
> What sliver of open space do I need to push through right now?
> What next step can I take with that sliver?

Don't just feedback, feed-forward

What you aren't aware of you can't change
Deepak Chopra, M.D.

Most organizations have pretty solid methods for evaluating the past. Online reviews, company-wide surveys, evaluations after an event and 360 degree evaluations are just a few. Solid feedback won't come to us as naturally as we'd like to think. Most people hold the truth back from leaders. They're not being deceptive; they're afraid. Leaders hold an accidental power dynamic. People on your team or in your company may not be intimidated by your personality, but your position holds weight. It's scary to tell the truth to someone who signs your paycheck. On top of this, people may really like you and see all the hard things you deal with as a leader. They don't want to hurt you so they choose to be "nice" and hold back the truth.

Others wait for complaints, but great leaders seek out feedback and make changes. The leader has to normalize and even incentivize a culture of feedback before people will offer it regularly. Feedback is helpful for analyzing our gaps and victories, but it's only half the story. Once you have feedback on how you did, it's time to start preparing for next time. Feedback should lead to feed-forward. Once we know where we can do better we can prepare for exactly how we will change next time.

Feedback looks back to see how we did.

Feed-forward looks ahead to make changes for next time.

Feedback asks, "How could I have done better?"

Feed-forward asks, "How will I specifically do better next time?"

Feedback can reveal how my team felt I moved too quickly on the project leading to disappointing results. Then I can sit with my team calmly and devise the plan for how I will partner better with them next time. That hard moment is the best time to form our future plan.

Feed-forward is a practical way for new awareness to shape new actions. It prepares us for new actions and new processes, quickly connecting the past to the future. If you want a greater impact or a healthier culture channel your energy toward the future instead of beating yourself up.

> **Reflect on feeding forward**
>
> What processes do I have for soliciting feedback on my leadership?
>
> How can I flip feedback processes into feed-forward processes?

Accept that you'll never be "over the hump"

*What we are waiting for is not as important
as what happens to us while we are waiting*
Mandy Hale

I was driving the curvy roads back from the Colorado high country with two friends and business leaders I deeply respect. We were filthy from clearing trees all day. Between the ripping chainsaws and "timberrrrrrrrrr!" warnings we talked on and off all day about our families, our hobbies, and our businesses.

"When will I get 'over the hump' in my business?" one of them asked. We listened with empathy for a full thirty seconds and shared that we were both at similar spots. Then the floodgates of sarcasm opened for all three of us. For twenty minutes we joked about this proverbial hump. *"Where is the hump?... I've gotta be close. I thought I was over it? Hump day?... I've been living in a hump decade! I quit at the last hump."* It was better than therapy.

What if there is no actual hump to get over? What if we're waiting for it to magically get easy, and that's just not going to happen? What if the problems don't go away, they only change? I know this sounds discouraging, but it can actually be helpful. Our broken thinking is actually creating unrealistic expectations that some day we'll just magically coast through life or leadership.

Parents have a gleam in their eye dreaming about a day when they won't have to wipe butts and tie shoes anymore, but then there are middle school hormones and the fun attitudes that accompany them. Founders dream of the day when the team will be big enough to "focus on our own lanes" and hire specialists, but then people issues will increase and meeting payroll will be downright scary. The nonprofit CEO dreams of the budget hitting $5 million so they can finally hire high caliber staff members, but then they have to keep raising that money year after year.

> Progress brings victories and problems. The trick is evaluating whether they're worth the tradeoff.

Last week two of my coaching clients talked about their versions of "over the hump".

"Over the hump" for one leader is finding four more paying clients so he can pay his bills and for the other leader is preparing his team to deliver on a $42 million dollar contract. Progress brings victories and problems. The trick is evaluating whether they're worth the tradeoff.

The ultimate "over the hump" moment for many founders is selling their business and walking away with millions. But this season actually creates deep insecurity and disorientation. Many owners feel lost and naked when they sell a business. Financial problems are fixed, but other issues come into focus.

If you're climbing mountains these are called false summits. As you peer up ahead they look like the peak, but they're just a big bump along the climb. You think you're just steps away from the summit only to realize you still have miles to go. False summits are a natural part of leading. Pause to rest, take a breather, look how far you've come, and keep moving toward your next one.

PART FOUR | Habits to keep you climbing

This is why it's so crucial to keep our purpose (our big WHY) in front of us. It helps us learn to love the process, not just the results. We are shaped through the pain and joy along the climb.

> **Reflect on your "over the hump" thinking**
>
> What "over the hump" moments do I fantasize about?
>
> What relief will those moments bring?
>
> What new problems will those moments create?

Create more than you consume

Choose better inputs. Get better outputs.
James Clear

It was early morning and I was walking the streets of New York City. The buildings were massive. The leaves in Central Park were ablaze. Fresh thoughts were popping into my head. I was experiencing the same thing flat-landers do when they come to the Rockies; pure awe. Finding the creative reset button needs to be a discipline for leaders.

We are designed to consume beauty and make it and to find meaning and make it. This is one reason sabbath is such a gift. After a week of output-ting we get to just be, to cease creating for anyone else. We pause from a week of duty to breathe in delight.

We can find ourselves equally worn down from our inputs and our outputs, what we create, and what we consume. One reason for the uptick in anxiety connected to social media is our habit of over-consuming and under-creating. If we spend more time watching illusions of beauty in others' lives than creating beauty we will dry up.

I've observed people who experience deep meaning in their lives create more than they consume. It's an act of resistance and the work of discipline. Their craft is connection, art, words, food or meaning. They create from desire and service, and others come to bask in their creations. They grow themselves and their craft so they can offer it to others.

I often get the question, "What books do you recommend about_____ (insert topic here)?" This is a good question, and I admire anyone who wants to learn. In fact, there is a list of recommended resources in the back of the book to dive deep on particular subjects. It's great to consume books, documentaries, podcasts or courses that challenge us. But it's only a start. Great leaders consume, and then create. They bring new things into the world. They practice in public. They put out rough drafts and learn from them, make them better, edit them, and release them. They keep learning and keep taking steps.

> Consuming without creating will leave us over-nourished and overwhelmed.

Learning is easy today. We have access to world-class content — from college courses to hands-on tutorial videos; master classes to books from the highest performers in the world. We can consume any of these while on a stationary bike or doing the dishes. Consuming without creating will leave us over-nourished and overwhelmed. The large conference market is in decline, because we no longer need to cross the country to consume the best content; it's on our phone. The greatest gatherings today are creating experiences that connect people. Those aren't going out of style anytime soon.

We will forget content, but experiences mark our lives. I have fond memories of swaying to the Lumineers with my wife at Red Rocks, ditching a conference to grab tacos with new friends and singing Sweet Caroline at karaoke with my nine year old daughter as the cruise ship lounge erupted "bomp bomp bomp!". Joseph Pine talks at length in his book *The Experience Economy* about how the great companies turn services into experiences. They create, even curate, experiences that bring us surprise and delight. Every leader has the opportunity to create meaningful experiences for those we serve.

Everyone has ideas, but those who turn them into experiences will shape the future. They will create moments, memories, connections, products, cultures, and meaning. As our team was forming I was reading about companies giving their employees days or weeks to work on new projects or develop themselves. With the limited funds we had, I designed a smaller version of that. I created an opportunity for one of our team members to attend a mountain retreat to clarify her purpose and calling. This experience cost less than a thousand dollars and a few days away from work, but it changed her life. Don't believe the lie that if you can't do it big for your employees you shouldn't do it at all.

I observed coaching clients taking five steps forward during coaching sessions, and two step backwards before our next session. I began dreaming of a journal that applied our coaching practices into daily and weekly form. My teammate, an apprentice and I invested months into studying other journals. Less than a year later we released a two week pilot and solicited feedback. Then we released the *Right Side up Journal* to the public. We listened even deeper for feedback, and made tweaks for Version two. At the time this book is releasing we just released our Third Edition of the *Right Side up Journal*. It's our best yet, because it's built on everything we've learned along the way. People are using it every morning to take steady steps. You don't have to boil the ocean; just take your next right step. Find a pain point and create what people need.

We learn as we create. If Apple has permission to get better with time, so do you. We realize our gaps and improve them for next time. Put the launch date on your calendar, and commit to it publicly. Take the risk before you feel like you're ready. Create a rough draft, and be ready to make revisions. When it's time to release it, promote it like crazy. No one will believe in what you've created more than you will.

Once you're known as someone who creates more than they consume, you'll be seen as valuable to people, teams and organizations. People will know you create valuable things, and they will ask you to create more valuable things with them. Whatever you do, don't get stuck consuming more than you create.

> **Reflect on creating**
>
> In which area of my life am I over-consuming instead of creating?
>
> What are the right inputs I need to consume?
>
> What things have I dreamed of creating?
>
> What is holding me back?

Order a Right Side up Journal **here**

Care more than everyone else

Caring for others is the highest expression of humanity
Harriet Beecher Stowe, Uncle Tom's Cabin

I thought I was going to puke right there in the driver's seat. I had stumbled out of a meeting with my CPA after organizing our company structure. The stakes felt so high, and I'm pretty sure the CPA was speaking Russian. I was so far out of my lane.

I was watching coaching clients transform their lives, but I had no idea about the business side of things. I didn't study business in college, and I had heard conflicting advice from people I respected. I had come down with a serious case of imposter syndrome. Everything in me was asking, "What are you even doing running a business?"

Turns out I'm not the only one. I work with a lot of leaders who feel like they're way out of their league, beyond their depth, in completely foreign terrain. Maybe they quickly launched a business, accidentally fell into their job or a friend promoted them for their character. And, like me, they have never been here before.

Over the years my confidence as an entrepreneur has grown slowly, but steadily. I wish I could tell you there was a magical day I felt I belonged as a coach and an entrepreneur, but that would be a big fat lie.

AntiBurnout

I still walk into rooms of amazing coaches and business leaders and wonder, "What am I even doing here?" Every coaching client brings new challenges, which is one reason I love coaching, and nearly every week I face a new business challenge. This is why mentors or frientors are vital; they've been where you want to go.

The next challenge is waiting on every wrung of leadership. When you choose the path of continual growth, new challenges will keep coming at you. This is why I coach some leaders for years and always have new things to talk about. Hungry leaders always have another dragon to slay.

> Care is a competitive advantage. It's hard to become great at your craft if you don't care about those you're serving.

During an initial Breakthrough Coaching Session, potential clients share the opportunities and obstacles they're facing. Many times I have not had technical experience in their industry, but I ask questions about their mindset, their approach and their next steps. Many of them tell me later that they chose me as their coach, because they knew I actually cared. Plenty of coaches and consultants have coached for longer than I have, but I have committed to care deeply about the health and success of every client. I bring my best, whether it's a paid session or I'm investing it into them. I focus on their growth goals before money. I give clients access to my cell and exchange video calls with them. I try my best to give feedback on documents and proposals between sessions. I write notes and text them encouragement at random times. Leadership can feel overwhelming and lonely, and if they invite me to climb mountains with them I am committed to care for them as deeply as I can.

Care is a competitive advantage. It's hard to become great at your craft if you don't care about those you're serving. People can smell if you care or not. In an increasingly automated world of AI, bots, and mass emails, care can separate you from the others.

PART FOUR | Habits to keep you climbing

During a hard season of my life I was carrying a lot of weight and shame around our finances. My wife and I had overdraft-ed several times in one month, and a bank manager called me to chat. I expected a scolding, but I got the opposite. She cared, I mean genuinely cared, that we were struggling. I began tearing up and shared the challenges of the season with her. There are plenty of places to do banking, but this conversation is one of the reasons we still bank there.

Caring deeply impacts us, too. When I made the commitment to care deeply for every client my energy and enthusiasm spiked. The pressure to grow a large coaching agency was dragging me down, but the personal interactions were charging me back up. I became more aware of how a mass email could find one person who desperately needed clarity and relief. My engagement with my clients rose, because I was more engaged. Not only was my care changing them, it was changing me.

I'm not saying experience and skills don't matter. It's important to be excellent in our craft. One way I care for my current and future coaching clients is by honing my coaching and leadership. I want to learn everything I possibly can about leadership and sharpening my tools so I can help them continue to ascend. Like an expecting mother I feel like I'm always eating for two. But technical skill doesn't always win over care. I hope my airline pilot has both, but I choose to fly on Southwest instead of Frontier, because they actually care. And they're having fun doing it.

Is it possible to care too much? Of course it is! Boundaries, margin, and rest are vital, especially if you are in a caregiving industry. My wife serves in the incredible and challenging field of foster care. Sometimes she fields calls late at night to place kids in transition with loving families who will provide them refuge. In order to continue caring about her work, she has to create and hold boundaries. This is why lazy Saturdays are so vital to us, and we rarely do anything out of our home before 1PM on Saturday. Sometimes we put our heads on the pillow after a long day or week and say, "I'm tired, good tired". These are the times we've cared deeply and spent ourselves in ways that matter. It's simultaneously exhausting and fulfilling.

AntiBurnout

Don't hide behind technical jargon, degrees on your wall or a fancy website. Invest as much energy as you can in out-caring everyone else.

> **Reflect on your care**
>
> How much do I care about my work right now (1-10)?
>
> How has that number changed over the past months or years? Why has it changed?
>
> What is one practice I can add to express care to those I serve?

View sales as an invitation

"Invite, don't sell"
Will Guidara, World renowned restaurateur[68]

Most people have a lot of baggage about selling. I'm sure you've experienced leaders who tricked you into a business lunch, sold their vision too hard or wouldn't take no for an answer. We all fear being the used care salesman. In fact, my daughter got sucked into a dirty deal on a used car that's still impacting her.

We want to be so far from being "that guy" that we refuse to promote what we've painstakingly created. It can cause us to resist selling or hope others magically discover our product, book or non-profit. Don't let your baggage from a few interactions hold you back from inviting others to change their lives. If this anti-sales mindset isn't corrected, organizations will cease to exist and rob others of the transformation you can bring.

Many leaders feel the weight of constantly selling their ideas, their services, their products or their vision. If the pressure of selling is wearing you down pick up another tool; invitation. When you create something, a vital part of the process is inviting people to invest in it. One of the greatest wordsmiths and sales trainers on the globe,

AntiBurnout

Phil M. Jones, sums up the process of selling into one thing: inviting people into conversations[69]. Convincing people to participate in new things with their time or money is about connection, not coercion.

What do you need to invite others to invest in? If you need volunteers, invite them to change lives through this serving opportunity. If you sell products, invite them to improve their lives by investing in it. If you poured your heart into writing a book invite us to buy it. I hope this book was more valuable than taking a friend to Chipotle. If not shoot me an email, and I'll Venmo you a refund. My email is in the front of the book. If you need to raise funds, invite a potential donor into a conversation about how this money will change lives. If you don't believe in what you're selling, go sell something else. But if you know it changes lives, keep inviting people to be part of it.

> If the pressure of selling is wearing you down pick up another tool; invitation.

Whenever I invite someone to a social event or leadership experience I'm hosting I say, "You're always invited, but never expected". People appreciate dignifying invites even if they don't come. If people aren't turning you down you're not inviting enough people. Don't take it personally when people say no or never respond. It likely has nothing to do with you. They're probably overwhelmed with responsibilities and trying to keep their head above water. Often people show no indication they're interested and suddenly they show up, buy, or give. Maybe their perspective, circumstances or schedule changed.

One leader asked me to include him on invitations to gatherings. He never responded to my texts, but I kept him on the invite list. Eventually he showed up to a backyard gathering I hosted and shared how his marriage was on the rocks and he desperately needed environments like this. He apologized for ghosting me and thanked me for not giving up on him.

It's personal. It stings when people don't buy, give, or show up. Our job is to clearly invite, others job is to respond. If you want to keep leading you won't graduate from invitation. As you ascend as a leader the invitations get bigger. If you want to continue impacting people you're going to have to find your flavor of invitation.

> **Reflect on invitation**
> In which area do I feel the greatest weight of selling?
>
> How can reframing sales to invitations take pressure off?
>
> What are the next invitations I will give?

Cultivate empowerment, not dependency

Leadership is not about being in charge.
Leadership is about taking care of those in your charge.
Simon Sinek

The bus snaked through the dusty, winding roads and came to a stop. I was nervous about what we would encounter and sad at the poverty I observed. I was nervous to get off the bus. Just a few years earlier I had experienced less-than-dignifying dependency on outside aid in another country visit. What I experienced those few days was not what I anticipated. The children had joy in their eyes, and the community leaders had pride in their hearts. There were no unusual signs of outside aid, only local heroes who were serving their local community with excellence. I could smell the scent of empowerment.

Dependency diminishes people, empowerment expands them. When we empower people we remind them they have the creativity and resources to succeed. Dependency leaves others believing they don't have the resources to succeed, so they must rely on others from the outside[70]. We need to help others in need, but we can do this with dignity that creates empowerment.

Leaders can serve from a dependency mindset or an empowerment mindset. The boss who leads with dependency believes she is vital to the success of every project, and she must create all the solutions. She accidentally diminishes the autonomy and engagement of the team through her lack of trust. But the boss who leads with empowerment believes the team has what they need to succeed. She collaborates and supports the team, but she trusts the team to deliver what they said they would. Empowering leaders offer trust that makes people bring their best.

Leaders with an empowerment mindset equip others with the skills they need to succeed, and let them test themselves along the way. Leaders with a dependency mindset believe all the answers have to come from the top of the org chart, and cannot be generated from within each department. We often accidentally create dependency. Our fear, anxiety, or insecurity sabotages us. Instead of trying to influence people, we seek to control them. Our underlying beliefs leak out in the heat of the moment.

One reason I became a coach is because I believe in human potential to change and create new solutions. God has given each of us the agency to create and design beautiful and functional things. I love supporting others well and leaving them feeling empowered to act and move. I believe people can grow and change, and I offer that mindset as a gift to my clients.

Take some time to look for signs of dependency or empowerment in you, your organization, and your team. Awareness is the first step toward new action. Look for signs, ask questions and be a student of what is going on inside of meetings, and organizational charts, and team project flows.

Reflect on an empowerment mindset

In what ways do I accidentally create dependency instead of empowerment?

What underlying belief causes me to do that?

What area would I like to create greater empowerment in others?

What is my first step toward that?

Work from rest, don't rest from work

Rest is salvation. It pulls you back from the edge and replenishes the emptiness of daily pouring out.[71]
Saundra Dalton Smith, M.D.

In my late twenties I came to the end of myself. I had talent and drive, but life simply required more than I knew how to give. I had two young kids and new opportunities at work. Turning up the dial a little higher wasn't working anymore. Out of sheer exhaustion, I uncovered the only path forward, a weekly sabbath. In my faith tradition Sabbath is a vital principle. Simply put, sabbath is a day to stop producing and simply…be.

I had dabbled in a weekly sabbath before then, but I finally surrendered to it. My wife has always been better at resting than me. These days gave my wife and I one big exhale. We allowed ourselves to breathe deep, take in beauty and enjoy good things. I tried to keep them free from email, work tasks and commitments. On these beautiful days my optimism rose, and my stress receded. I felt more connected to my wife and kids, and I was more pleasant to be around (my wife verified this). I realized I had needs, and I paused to meet them. I also began producing more and better work. My thinking was clearer, and I felt more purpose in my work.

This has been my regular practice for many years now. On these days I remember I'm a human again, not just a leader and certainly not a machine. On sabbath days the cappuccino tastes better, the sun seems warmer, the couch feels cozier, and my thinking is sharper. As leaders and parents we get stuck in the "have-to's" of meeting everyone's needs. We rarely get to pause and savor the "get to's". Sabbath is a "get-to" day in a "have-to" world.

Sabbath has a rich history. God rested from creating the world not because He needed it, but because He knew we would. He was modeling it for us. Then the Israelites, who were enslaved to Egypt, followed suit taking one day to rest from their grueling labor. Both the principle and practice of Sabbath have sustained the Jewish people for millennia.

This old practice is a breath of fresh air in our anxiety-driven, white-knuckle, go-til-you-drop culture. If you wait to rest until you have the time, you'll never do it. In our culture, we work until we can't anymore. Then we crash. Resting is not crashing. When we get into this work/crash cycle we have nothing left to offer our families and communities. If every week ends at minus 5 then a great weekend only gets us back up to minus 1. We're still living at a deficit. Then we do it on repeat week after week. This cycle has us perpetually living on defense.

Until we view rest as essential to life we will continue to over-work. We must change the paradigm from resting from work to working from rest. Rest is essential to life, to work and to being human. It is possible to live at or below your capacity each week, get true rest, and be ready to take on another week. If we want to produce great work we must learn the art of resting well.

Please know I'm a fellow struggler here. I've run myself ragged several times, and I still resist rest sometimes. I understand what a full life feels like. On a normal week you'll find me running businesses, driving my kids to evening activities, showing up for my friends, squeezing in runs to the grocery store, taking on new projects and making time for hobbies. My wife works a very demanding job, and we share family responsibilities. I am trying to seize these precious years with my four kids. I want to steward my responsibilities, serve others well, and be emotionally available to my family. Like you, if I don't fight for rest, it won't naturally appear. I want you to experience a sustainable life, not the weight of unrealistic expectations. I want to be clear. Here's what I believe about rest.

Resting is not inaction, it is a powerful action.
Resting is not a bonus, it is a necessity.
Resting is not escape, it is engagement.
Resting is not a waste, it is wisdom.
Resting is not selfish, it is caring for you and those around you.
Resting is not crashing, it is preparation.
Resting is not an expense, it is an investment.
Resting is not quitting, it is resisting.

A sabbatical is an extension of Sabbath. This concept is foreign to some and familiar to others. I define a sabbatical as "a month or more away from your primary work with the purpose of replenishment and the intention to come back stronger." It is usually administered by an organization for a leader to replenish, direct energy into others places and reconnect with their family. Sometimes a person is between jobs or sells their company and designates their own sabbatical season. It usually results in renewed vision for the future. Some leaders dream of a sabbatical, others are terrified by the idea. This time away from work can expose a leader's over-reliance on work and reveal gaps in their identity. When leaders don't plan well for sabbatical it can be destructive, but with some planning it can be a turning point of a leader's life, family and leadership. Many leaders have told me their careful planning and wise navigation of sabbatical gave them vision for the next decade of life and leadership. A few have told me it saved their their marriage.

I experienced two sabbaticals at just the right times. These were two of the greatest gifts I've ever received. This time away from work allowed me to reconnect with my family, gave my soul space to catch up and helped me lift my eyes to the future. With help from books and others who had experienced a sabbatical, I mustered the best plans I could heading into my first sabbatical. I give my first sabbatical a C–. Years later, I implemented what I learned, and the next one was a C+. I needed a Sabbatical Coach, but I didn't know to look for one. They could've helped me navigate, normalize and learn from the disorientation I was experiencing.

Years later I find myself doing nearly as much Sabbatical Coaching as Leadership Coaching. I get to help leaders plan before a sabbatical (I call this the Prepare Phase), navigate the joy and disorientation of sabbatical (I call this the Experience Phase) and transform their life rhythms as they head back to work (I call this the Reorient Phase).

True rest only happens proactively. If you want to prioritize what matters to you and do excellent work learn to rest. Time away from work, whether it's two days or two months, gives us the space to re-examine our priorities as we stop producing. Even if you never take more than a long vacation you can prioritize rest every week. I invite you to create habits of rest that allow you to enjoy life, prioritize your family, and work hard. I promise you, it's possible.

> **Reflect on rest**
> How tired am I right now? (1-10)
>
> What are my broken beliefs about rest?
>
> What small activities are most restful for me?
>
> What could I experience from a weekly Sabbath day?

Optimize your schedule (especially your meetings)

A well-designed life is a life that is generative.
You get out of it more than you put in.
Bill Burnett and Dave Evans[72]

A friend asked me for some help tweaking his work schedule. I felt claustrophobic as he walked through his typical week crammed with one-on-ones. A nonprofit leader shared how meeting overload was wearing her whole team down. They were already overloaded with work, and the boss would hold three hour emergency "all hands on deck" meetings. A business leader told me he came to work dreading his meeting load every week. It was pushing him out of his genius zone of solving big problems and cultivating organizational culture. I hear too many stories like this. Most leaders schedules need a serious overhaul.

Whenever a leader is concerned about their energy level, I start by auditing their meetings. Most teams are paying a hefty price for meeting overload. Perhaps I'll write a whole book about this in the future; I'm that concerned about it. Too many organizations are setting their leaders up to be continually drained by meetings while simultaneously blocking their greatest contributions and energy flow.

Somehow we've gotten the idea that meetings create results. I call this "meeting dependency" (sounds better than a meeting addition, right?). I believe this is rooted in insecurity and control. If we don't believe we're getting enough done, or we don't believe the team is getting enough done, we add more meetings to check in. Dr. Henry Cloud says, "Just getting together does not bring unity, as bad meetings have shown us all."[73] Over-reliance on meetings drains massive energy and breaks up our schedule into small blocks. Most teams would be better served to have less meetings that are more focused.

If you're experiencing meeting overload, here are some specific ways to find relief and optimize your meetings.

Eliminate all non-vital meetings. If you don't know why the meeting exists, and it's not a necessity. Get rid of it.

Turn potential meetings into an email or a short conversation. Whenever someone goes up the organizational chart, they tend to ask for a meeting. Before you accept their request ask, "Do you have a specific question I can answer?" That email or short interaction can save both of you time.

Cut the number of recurring meetings in half. Shift from weekly meetings to every-other-week instead. This often increases their quality.

Cut your meeting time in half. Limitation breeds innovation. It's especially true with meetings. If you only have thirty minutes you will utilize the time better. This naturally focuses the meeting.

Create an agenda, follow it and force preparation. Creating and following a meeting agenda values everyones' time and allows people to prepare. Following a regular cadence for meetings creates momentum and psychological safety.

Dismiss the meeting when you're done. If you've covered the agenda or people feel disengaged release the hounds. Sometimes you declare the meeting over, and people hang around, joke and create meaningful connections.

If you follow these steps you can open up as much as a full day every week. Increase the focus of meetings and you'll increase the focus of the team. Be gently ruthless with meetings. View new commitments as "guilty until proven innocent." If we are wasting peoples hours, we are wasting their lives. Meetings aren't the enemy. Un-dignifying, un-clarified, un-focused meetings are the enemy. Billions of hours are wasted every single year in meetings. Think what we could be doing with that extra time!

Almost everyone I meet wants to design their lives for impact, but few leaders have designed their weekly schedule for impact. If you want to increase your effectiveness start by reexamining your schedule. The higher a leader rises on an organizational chart, the more responsibility they have to limit organizational clutter. Most people have limiting beliefs about their time that are working against their needs and their values. Here are mental shifts that can help you think differently about your schedule.

> Be gently ruthless with meetings. View new commitments as "guilty until proven innocent."

Your schedule isn't locked; it's fluid.
You have more autonomy of your time than you think.
If you think like a designer your schedule can work for your priorities.
You are likely the one holding you back, not your boss or organization.
Working against your schedule creates energy loss, but working with your schedule creates energy gain.

I have overhauled my schedule several times. The results have included adding large creative blocks, ending work earlier, exercising during the work day, making space for naps, dedicating time to big projects, taking Fridays off, and batching similar tasks on similar days. Optimizing my schedule has given me the mental clarity to wear different hats without getting overwhelmed and still showing up well for my family. I used to reexamine my schedule annually, then it moved twice a year, but now I tweak it quarterly.

Remember, the currency of leadership is energy, not time. We aren't just shaving time; we're saving energy. Some meetings cost more energy than others. I experience video calls to be 1.5x or 2x more tiring than in-person meetings. Depending on your wiring, you may love or hate meetings about details, dreaming, strategy or goal planning. We can't skip every meeting we don't like, so budget your energy appropriately.

It's time to get creative. Perhaps you can batch meetings together on a few days a week, and save the other days for self-paced projects. Maybe it's time to reevaluate the purpose of each recurring meeting. You may decide to add a communication channel throughout the week that could be more effective than that meeting.

> **Reflect on your schedule**
>
> If I had a magic wand what would I do to my schedule?
>
> What parts of my schedule are working for me?
>
> What parts are working against me?
>
> What would I like to design my schedule to have more of?
>
> What needs to change about my meeting rhythm?

Learn to live whelmed

Never train your horse to exhaustion. Leave him wanting more.
Thoroughbred Horse Trainer

I lived most of my twenties five minutes late. I packed my schedule full, sliding pieces in wherever I could like Tetris. In fact, my propensity to over-leverage time was the source of my first fight with my wife. Needless to say, it wasn't working great for me. I would walk into meetings unprepared while glancing at my phone. I would often realize I was unprepared for a big project or deadline the day before. Many Sunday nights I wanted a weekend do-over. I was last-minute and lazy. I was living overwhelmed, but I didn't know another way.

Many leaders live constantly overwhelmed with bloated schedules, inboxes, and task lists. When there is no margin, the only option is to make the treadmill go faster. While a level of stress brings us to peak performance, too much stress is dangerous. Our bodies aren't meant to live off constant adrenaline pumping through our veins or caffeine shots helping us survive the next meeting.

Leaders, I hate to tell you this, but we're a bit strange. We are people of extremes. We can relish the adrenaline rush of a deadline (or several at the same time), feel energized by being behind and prefer busyness to moderation. We normalize overwhelm with phrases like *"riding the rocket," "busting a hump," "running like crazy,"* and *"just trying to keep my head above water".* We compare notes with other leaders and get the idea that success requires living continually past our limits. This doesn't work as well as we think it does.

When exhaustion overtakes us, we get overwhelmed. We swing the pendulum and quit, hold back, or play small. Sometimes it feels like the only alternative to living overwhelmed is living underwhelmed. In this state we under-live our lives and miss opportunities in front of us. We hold back from making an impact all the while getting a gnawing sense we're wasting our potential.

What if there was another option besides overwhelm or underwhelm?
What if we could live whelmed?

It is, indeed, possible to live and lead whelmed. Whelmed leaders look at each week ready to bring their best without pushing past their limits. They know themselves and have learned to leverage their unique design to multiply value to others. But, like many third options, living whelmed feels impossible at first. In moments of stress, our brains corner us into binary choices, "either/or" decisions. It's tempting to feel like we have to be all in or all out. This may require revisiting your fundamental views of work. Perhaps you learned from full-throttle leaders, have used work to self-medicate or worked in dysfunctional cultures. Maybe you've just never seen healthy leadership modeled.

I want to invite you to find a middle gear between sprinting and stalling. This is not a problem to be solved, but a tension to be managed. An effective leader functions at a sustainable pace, and others are looking to them as the pacesetter. It requires discernment each week and each season. Healthy habits are the pathway to this middle ground of living and leading whelmed. Making proactive decisions ahead of time can help you take ground at a sustainable pace. I recommend some helpful habits for the long climb at the end of the book.

PART FOUR | Habits to keep you climbing

Reflect on leading whelmed

What situations tend to push me toward overwhelm?

What situations tend to push me toward underwhelm?

What will I have to resist in order to live whelmed?

Ditch hype, cultivate hope

Transformation happens when hope takes root and continues to flourish
Adam Forerer and Elliott Connie, Therapists

"What's worth doing even if you fail?"[74] This arresting question has invited me to take three major risks over the last decade. I'm currently in the middle of one of those. I've been burdened by the loneliness epidemic that has blanketed our world. I've always been fascinated by creating spaces where people connect, collaborate, and create beautiful things. Over the last few years, I've observed that working from home isn't actually working for most people.

I am partnering with a few friends to create hub spaces and ecosystems across the country that bring communities together (think coworking meets and event space meets marketplace). The idea had been germinating in my friend, Jeremiah, since he was a teenager. Now, our work is expanding, but at one point this was only an idea without a space or a community. During the prototyping, soft launch, and the launch phases the dream felt fragile. Every week I wondered, "Is this going to work?". The problem seemed overwhelming and the barriers seemed impossible. But the reality of the loneliness epidemic grounds me. This is worth doing even if we fail.

AntiBurnout

We are enduring a slow leak of hope in our culture today. We see a handwritten note in the mail only to realize it's from an insurance company. We watched social media platforms morph from connection to grenade launching. We hear another court case of corporate greed end with a slap on the wrist. We believe a candidate can bring change only to realize they've been coopted by the political machine. We see atrocities on the news with no way to respond. We go to lunch with a new friend only to realize it was a sales meeting. We join a new church hoping it will be our permanent place of worship, but we don't find a connection. We have big projections for the product launch, but they fall short. We hope the board will fire the CEO who is mistreating the staff only to see them let it blow over. We see another scandal in our news feed. We abandon watching the news just to stay sane. These hope leaks are breaking us down.

People feel let down by systems like government, religion and family. Everyone seems outraged by something. Our world seems more depersonalized with the rise of mass everything. Our ability to believe things can be different is eroding slowly. We are in a crisis of hope. How do we find lightness in these heavy days?

> People are done with hype, but hungry for hope. Hype and hope are only one letter off, but they are worlds apart.

We've tried to swap hope for a cheap replacement: hype. This "death by a thousand paper cuts" is making us resistant, even allergic to, hype. When we're already exhausted it's hard to believe the next product, idea, or change will be worth it. The barrage of marketing is wearing down our souls. This violence to our souls is an invitation to rest, another reason a sabbath may be more vital right now more than ever.

People are done with hype, but hungry for hope. Hype and hope are only one letter off, but they are worlds apart. Hype is not the same thing as marketing. I'm all for good marketing. We must boldly share the things we've created if they are going to make an impact. I'd go far enough to say if you create something that brings goodness, beauty, or truth you have a responsibility to help others find it. Marketing is not the problem. Broken promises that were never meant to fulfill us are the problem. Hype is a broken promise waiting to happen.

Hype makes us believe something will quickly solve our problem.
Hope makes us believe it's worth doing the hard work of change.
Hype is shared externally.
Hope is cultivated internally.
Hype is cheap.
Hope is costly.
Hype convinces us to buy for the short-term gain.
Hope invites us invest for the long-term tradeoff.

People are desperately searching for hope-filled leaders. Leaders who do the private, deep, internal work will be able to offer hope to others. Erwin McManus says, *"Optimism is a discipline"*.[75] Hope will leak accidentally, and it must be cultivated intentionally. Eventually hype gets found out to be flimsy, but true hope cultivates more hope. Hype will not shape the future, but hope will.

> **Reflect on hope**
> How high is my hope level right now? (1-10)
>
> What big or small things erode my hope?
>
> What do I believe is worth hoping in right now?
>
> What practices regularly cultivate my hope and optimism?

Create the safety to risk (and fail)

> *If leaders really want people to show up, speak out, take chances,
> and innovate, we have to create cultures where people feel safe.*
> Brené Brown[76]

In leadership circles we talk a lot about about innovation, but we rarely define what it takes to cultivate environments that breed innovation. Environments that perpetually innovate hold a tension between risk and safety, chaos, and order. Dee Hock of Mastercard calls this paradox *chaordic*. In order to risk humans must know they have the freedom to make calculated failures. Fear pops up and scares us away from risk. Many world-changing ideas will go to the grave with people, because they never felt safe to share them.

How do we know if an idea is great or a dud? We have to test them. If you want to test an idea don't aim for perfect; aim for prototype. Prototypes allow us to experiment our way into the future with the safety to know we don't have to get it right the first time. I naturally think like a designer, but I realize many people do not. Tim Brown's book, *Change by Design*, is helpful in framing a design process for innovating. He says, "Prototyping should start early in the life of a project, and we expect them to be numerous, quickly executed and pretty ugly."[77] Did you catch the three check boxes for prototypes? Numerous, quick and ugly. This low bar creates safety to make mistakes along the way.

Leaders need to get comfortable prototyping their way forward. So do organizations. Brown says, "When it comes to organizations, constant change is inevitable and everything is a prototype".[78] When the bar is lowered we can do what former Apple product designer Bill Burnett calls "sneaking up on the future".[79]

A few years ago I realized I had done a good job of creating a culture of risk and experimentation on our team, but I had done a poor job of creating safety. I worked with our team to create a document for our Stay Forth team called "How We Roll". I sought to clarify guardrails for how we interact with one another and with clients. The moment we released it I felt freedom, and others felt safety. It gives both permission and boundaries. We review it as a team occasionally, and give it to potential team members we are interviewing to warn them about our unique culture in advance. I encourage every team or organization to create something like this describing the rules of engagement.

Learning happens largely through experience. As Seth Godin reminds us, "No one learns to ride a bike from a manual."[80] Leadership classes and courses will only take you so far. You've got to get some bruises along the way in order to learn. We learn as we iterate and we iterate as we learn. If you're going to do anything significant, you'll have to take risks. It's important to know these are measured risks that won't cost you your job. You're going to send plenty of mass emails with typos and publish plenty of web pages you need to correct later. Everyone does. You won't get it perfect the first time, and some rough drafts will be rougher than others.

My iteration process

I've gotten pretty comfortable with risk over the years, but I still fear launching crap into the atmosphere. I've learned the beauty of creating prototypes and processes to refine ideas. Here's the process I've developed for prototyping and launching anything new.

Version 1 is a sketch or an idea map. I almost always do this in my journal. Paper feels safer than screens. At this point, it's either potential or crap. I don't which at first, so I sketch it and leave it.

Version 2 is an edited version. I take a second pass a few days later, sifting through my sketches, and I either chuck them or modify them. If it has potential I rework it, edit it, give it a name, and send it along to someone who can edit or digitize it.

Version 3 is a rough digital diagram or excerpt. I can begin testing this idea, article or tool in limited environments. It may be helpful to others, but I know it's not done. I show it to early adopters who can give me feedback, or I share the article with a small group.

> If you want to test an idea don't aim for perfect; aim for prototype.

Version 4 is a (nearly) complete tool or article. It's ready to share with coaching clients or a small audience. I have tweaked it, and it looks beautiful, but I know I'll need to make more small tweaks at some point. I have to practice in public with the ideas or tools watching how they play in the real world. At this point I'm looking for small final changes in order to maximize clarity and impact. People may give me small suggestions or ideas to make it better.

Version 5 is the final-ish product. It's what everyone gets to see, and I assume it's done. It looks pretty, I've gotten plenty of feedback on it, and I trust it. I use it with confidence sharing it however I can, because I've seen it help people. If it's an online resource, like a podcast episode, I send it to people whenever that topic surfaces in a conversation. Let the share-ability of the internet work for you, so it can impact as many people as possible.

Most people can follow a similar process. The best in the world don't graduate from a process of iterating, and they're always practicing in public. Comedians test their lines many times before we see it on the big stage. Without a prototyping process your perfectionism will swallow your next idea, and you'll never get the feedback you need to maximize it. If you want to create new things, start by cultivating the safety to risk and fail. Then develop a process you can continue using.

AntiBurnout

Reflect on creating safety to risk

How do I reward risk?

What is my definition of failure?

What is my iteration process?

View your limits as a gift

*Obstacles are those frightful things you see when
you take your eyes off your goal*
Henry Ford

My wife and I went from no kids to a six year old and two year old overnight through the miracle of adoption. About a year later my wife birthed our third child while she was still finishing her Master's degree. Our lives were full, and they got even fuller. It forced me to change how I did almost everything. I assumed I would lose influence during that season, because I had less time to invest in people. But the opposite happened. My influence increased. The limitations of this season forced me to think differently about my time and energy.

I had to shift from an addition mindset to a multiplication mindset. During the next few years I learned how to impact more people in less time while still investing in my family. Of no choice of their own, my kids have accidentally forced me to get clear on my priorities and get good at saying no to non-essentials. They have given me the beautiful gift of limitations.

Limitation breeds innovation. In design thinking limits are called constraints. Ironically, every project needs constraints in order to flourish. In our culture of excess, the lie is that the more we have, the more we can create. It's hard to stay grateful for your life if you aren't grateful for your limits. Our limited time, energy, and availability might not squelch your innovation; it might actually drive it. It sounds counterintuitive to think about limits as a gift, but they are.

It's easy to believe our limitations will snuff out our impact. We've all seen plenty of organizations fail due to lack of finances, but plenty of organizations have also failed to innovate because they were over-resourced. They lacked the urgency to "innovate or die." Those organizations often die a slow death of the heart while scrappy organizations innovate their way forward.

Time functions the same way. Projects grow to the deadline we give them. At first I wondered if the deadlines for this book were unreasonable. They were considerably shorter than my past writing deadlines, but they were ample to get the job done. I found time in cracks of my life BECAUSE of the shorter deadline. The limits became my stimulant.

Your awareness of your limited capacity could drive you to invite a team around you. If you don't have the time, energy or gifts necessary to do it all you can invite a team to help. A realization of your limits paired with the humility to ask for help can become the foundation for an engaged team.

Beware of thinking you need more time, energy, or capital than you actually do to move forward. Once you have enough to proceed, design the pathway. Take the steps. Build your way forward.

> **Reflect on your limitations**
>
> What is one personal or organizational limitation that's frustrating me right now?
>
> What is the opportunity for innovation below this?
>
> What limitation in my past turned into an opportunity?

Remember what got you here won't get you there

People only change their ways when what they truly value is threatened
Marshall Goldsmith, World-renowned Executive Coach

What got you into your current role? Charisma? Connections? Hard work? Technical knowledge? A head start? Brilliant ideas? Natural gifting? A great interview? The skills, hard work, and connections that got you where you are today won't get you where you want to go.

"*What got you here won't get you there.*"[81]. I say this to a coaching client at least twice a week. Perhaps this phrase brings a sigh of relief, because you're ready to exit a hard season. Perhaps it evokes fear of what the future holds. The things that helped you succeed in the past can drag you down in the future. Over-relying on your past is a sure way to under-live your future.

When I was newbie to professional coaching, I worked with a lot of leaders for cheap. If they seemed interesting to work with I tried to say yes. I needed to grow my coaching skills through repetition and unique challenges. Over the years I honed my craft and discovered which leaders I could serve best. After moving from a part-time coach to a full-time coach, I could no longer offer discounts like I had before. I developed filters for the kind of leaders I would coach, and the ones who weren't a great fit. I added much more value and experienced much more fulfillment through coaching leaders than I had before. I moved from a season of "gaining experience" to a season of "focus." I'm grateful for that early season, but staying there would've stunted my growth and held me back from paying my bills. We need to honor the actions, habits and mindsets that got us here without staying stuck in them.

> The things that helped you succeed in the past can drag you down in the future. Over-relying on your past is a sure way to under-live your future.

Leading is not a game. We're not taking a walk in the park. We're cutting through underbrush in the wilderness. We must remain humble learners in order to survive and thrive as leaders. We've all heard stories of pride and apathy crippling leaders and organizations. We're in danger of focusing on the rear view mirror and missing the curves ahead.

Thought leader and researcher Adam Grant says people are looking to follow those who live in a crucial tension: *"confident humility."*[82] I agree. We can simultaneously be humbled by the challenge and confident of our ability. There is always another hill to climb, change to navigate, issue to address, and chasm to cross. But what about those leading at a whole different level? They're feeling it too. The more you stretch and push yourself the more insecure you feel at the next level.

You can simultaneously take a jump and wonder if it's going to fly. I call this emotion "terricited". Every significant jump I've taken has been marked by fear and self-doubt. Every single one. Leaders I respect in various fields have told me the same thing. A beautiful and unexplainable courage arises when we're submitted to risking for a mission bigger than ourselves.

Disorientation precedes maturity. Having your first child is beautiful and challenging. Organizational growth generates new excitement and new demands. Adding team members brings new life and new challenges. Midlife creates new tensions, losses, challenges, and opportunities. Success gets us what we thought we wanted, but often feels anticlimactic. I bet you're approaching some shifts that are completely natural, and completely disorienting.

Sustaining change

It's one thing to make a change. It's another thing to sustain that change. We've talked about habits and rhythms several times during the book. You'll have to develop long-lasting, health-producing rhythms in your life, leadership and organization if you want to develop long-lasting change. You'll also need to stay focused on a few other things. Utilize the tool on the next page to help you prepare for sustainable change. If you are going to continue growing as a leader continue to pursue these five things: *new wisdom*, *new experiences*, *new relationships*, *new rhythms*, and *new metrics*. They will help you get where you want to go.

Whatever got you here is good; be thankful for it. But it won't get you to the heights you're going to.

> **Reflect on change**
>
> What do I need to stop doing in order to experience greater health and impact?
>
> What do I need to start doing?
>
> What change is most disorienting right now?

AntiBurnout

STAY FORTH: LASTING CHANGE BLUEPRINT

Hunger creates momentum for change, but these five things sustain it:

NAME

METRICS	RHYTHMS	RELATIONSHIPS	EXPERIENCES	WISDOM
What new things will you aim at and measure?	What actions will you regularly repeat?	Who do you need to learn from?	What new encounters do you need in order to grow?	What new information do you need to acquire?
How will you celebrate those victories?	When will you do these?	How will you learn from them?	How will you pursue those encounters?	How will you acquire it?

© Stay Forth Designs
Find more helpful tools at StayForth.com/resources

"Waste" time on a hobby

Idleness is, paradoxically, necessary to getting any work done [83]
Tim Kreider, Cartoonist

I was waist deep in freezing cold water laughing out loud. Every fly I casted looked like food to the rainbow trout that day. I walked back to my car grinning ear to ear from one of the best fishing days of my life. Sometimes I catch fish out there, sometimes I get my best ideas, and sometimes I just have fun. I don't think I'll ever become a professional fly fishing guide. I don't really want to.

I can't drive to a high mountain lake every week, so I pick up a design magazine next to the blazing wood stove or build something in my garage. I love doing light design projects, but I'll probably never be a professional designer. I just love sketching up a project and figuring out how to pull it off.

Hobbies can feel like a waste, but they're one of the best investments we can make. Hobbies fall into Stephen Covey's "important, but not urgent" category.[84] Hobbies remind us we care about other things than our job, and can help us take our minds off our work. A hobby is a non-essential activity you regularly practice simply for the enjoyment. Many things should stay in the "simply for enjoyment" category.

AntiBurnout

I knew a guy who turned his fly fishing hobby into a goal of catching 100 fish that year (#enneagram3). I took some guys fishing, and he was deeply bothered that the fish weren't biting that day. The rest of us just enjoyed being in the stream. We called it a day to enjoy a cold beer and a fine cigar on the bank.

Hobbies can provide the following.

Mental rest away from work

Fun

Replenishment of our energy

Distraction from weighty issues

Renewed passion for our family

Spikes in creativity

Solutions for problems we're trying to solve

Hobbies can bring lightness and buoyancy back to our lives. Try combining your needs and passions like exercise, outdoors, fun and social connection. It might be time to accept the invite to the biking club, frequent trivia night, plan the fishing excursion or join the book club you've been thinking about just for the enjoyment of it.

It's easy to fall out of touch with hobbies. The weight of responsibility at work and at home can push hobbies aside. When we feel maxed out at work and at home, and when money is tight, hobbies are the easiest thing to cut. But if you ignore them you're missing out on joy and replenishment. Don't be fooled; hobbies are way too important to ignore.

> **Reflect on hobbies**
>
> What hobbies do I want to resurrect?
>
> What is the most ideal hobby for me in this season of life?
>
> Which hobbies combine my desires and my needs?

Go slow or go fast, but don't rush

To truly make progress on the things that matter,
we need a whole new way to work and live.
Greg McKeown[85]

"What's the rush?" I asked this question in the most caring way I could to the couple sitting on my red overstuffed couch. They were about to upend their lives, move across the country, and launch their dream. Their stress and fear were contagious. After fifteen minutes of chipping away, the husband said to me, "It feels like now or never. We'll be too old in a few years." We examined this statement, and he reframed his thinking. They slowed down their process, waited a few years and moved to another state to launch a different dream. This beautiful family is thriving today.

Sometimes slow is good. Many times the issue is not that we have chosen the wrong thing, but that we have underestimated how long it will take to get there. We pressurize ourselves, our ideas, and our businesses to launch quickly. We want to create something amazing, but we don't want to take the time to develop it. We want to succeed in a new career, but we're not willing to hone our craft for a decade to get there. We're trying to cook crock pot meals in the microwave.

Intentionally slowing down can feel like detention. It's painful to feel like you're burning daylight on your dream while everyone else is maximizing it. You convince yourself the ideas simply can't wait. If you are set on launching something quickly identify your belief underneath your desire to go faster and evaluate it.

There's a difference between *wisely slow* and *fearfully slow*. Slowing down because of fear isn't wisdom; it's cowardice. I've missed opportunities because I was petrified. Other times I've made wise decisions to wait for the product or idea to mature. I waited three years to start writing this book until I knew I was ready, and then I moved quickly.

Sometimes the creative act is supposed to remain private. I wrote a novel that was deeply compelling to me as I wrote it. Half way through I realized it was actually an alternative storyline of my life, and I was basically creating a two hundred page journal entry. I see no need to publish it, but it was a gift to me. Other times it's wise to wait while we actively prepare ourselves for the right moment. There are no rules on timing, and discernment is always required.

Sometimes fast is good. Some moments and seasons carry momentum or gravitas that we can tap into. Wise leaders make use of rest and momentum, fast and slow, the inhale and the exhale. Sometimes ideas are timely and we must strike when the proverbial iron is hot. Some of the best podcast ideas we've had came together in ten minutes. Others took a year.

Some organizations made quick changes when COVID-19 shut our world down. The unique challenges of that moment created unique opportunities. We rode the wave and pulled off our first, and only, online summit with around five thousand attendees. We quickly learned new technology and partnered with a large organization to pull off a valuable event. If we would've waited we would've missed the wave.

Slow can be good, fast can be good, but rushed is bad. Sometimes you're going thirty miles over the speed limit desperately trying to make something work. When you're moving quickly pause and ask, "Is this fast or rushed?"

When we are rushed we tend to do the following.

Make unnecessary mistakes
Whip our teams into a frenzy
Compromise our values
Lower the excellence level
Push people aside
Avoid opportunities right in front of us

We've delayed projects over a year at Stay Forth, because life changed. If we get a sense we are rushing a project we will delay it. The primary emotion you will feel when you hit pause on a rushed idea is relief. Slowing down a rushed project also proves to your people they matter. Organizations that are constantly rushing and never pausing often end up experiencing culture drift.

We've never been able to gain success, name recognition or fame as quickly as we can today. It's scary. Careful of overnight success. The medium or audience you think is nurturing you can control you. What feels like a support can quickly become a weight around your neck. Go slow or go fast, but don't rush.

> **Reflect on your pace**
>
> Describe a time I caught a wave of momentum by moving quickly...
>
> What is one thing I or my team is rushing right now?
>
> How can I/we slow it down?

Don't forget people are the killer app

The currency of real networking is not greed but generosity
Keith Ferrazzi

Have you ever gotten stuck before you got started? It's a terrible feeling. Getting started on something we've never done can feel impossible. Next time you're experiencing failure to launch, look for a *who*, not a *what*. Instead of asking, "What information do I need?," try starting with, "Who has already been where I want to go?"

We tend to overestimate the information we need and underestimate the people we need. The right people will shortcut your time to reach your goals and skip over a lot of pain. Often, one cup of coffee, a zoom call, or a discussion with industry leaders can get you unstuck.

A question constantly runs like background music in my life: "How many people are one introduction away from breaking their barrier?" I get the incredible opportunity to connect people who can make each others dreams happen. Connecting two great people can create exponential impact. It can unlock something they could not unlock on their own. Two of my best friends met each other around a fire in my back yard. I introduced a coaching client to his hero before he died. I create environments each week that connect leaders who need comrades in our space. The right people can connect someone to their goals and to new networks. In a lonely, independent culture connection is the way forward. People are the killer app and the ultimate multiplier.

We tend to overestimate the information we need and underestimate the people we need.

Unfortunately, we've all had connections go poorly. Instead of connecting two sacred souls, we've had others transactional-ize this process. It stripped us of dignity, and left us gun shy. Our baggage from introductions gone wrong can hold us back from making true connections.

I recently co-led a learning intensive on connecting in our hub space. It was a mashup of a mastermind group, speed dating and a TED talk. I think the content my comrade and I brought was solid, but my favorite part was watching people pick a gift card from the pile and "ask someone out for a second date". People made genuine connections that day.

Here are my rules for connecting.

Give value to others before you ask for it back
Ask permission to connect them
Connect people quickly, but don't rush
Create an experience when connecting people
Underpromise and overdeliver when connecting people
Always save people's contact (it will be great to "know a guy" in the future)
When someone offers something great, keep following up until it's a yes or a no
Remember people's "dream connection" and try your best to connect them
Only share connections with people who have an abundance mindset

Instead of learning a new aspect of your business or continuing to struggle in an area, consider hiring someone. The right person, whether contractor, part-time, advisor, or full-time, can exponentially push you and your organization forward. Team members are partners, not resources. It's on us to trust them and give them clarity, and it's on them to deliver results. We must give trust first if we hope to see people thrive. Dan Sullivan is a master of this. I highly recommend his book *Who Not How* if you want to strategically grow your team.

I believe in paying people for the value they bring, not the time they work. The value they bring is greater than the time they work. When a team member feels valued, they bring their best work and contribute in multiple areas. Engaged employees advise other teams, mentor younger leaders, spark innovation, and create company culture that boosts retention. The " trade your time for money" model is antiquated and rewards slow work. It demotivates people, kills desire, and incentivizes laziness.

A skilled worker has cultivated a valuable skill, and that deserves good compensation and freedom. It has likely taken them hundreds of hours and various roles to gain these skills. Give them trust, give them clarity, set them free, and watch them multiply value. But if you don't value them, they will go somewhere their talent and creativity are welcome.

> **Reflect on valuing people**
>
> What issues am I stuck on? How can others get me unstuck?
>
> What environments help me connect with and learn from others?
>
> What are some specific ways I can show more trust to those under my care?

Build your process.
Then trust it.

Patience does not mean to passively endure.
It means to be farsighted enough to trust the end result of a process.
Elif Shafak

As I write these words I remember the fear I experienced writing my first book. I drained a bunch of energy fighting off the fear gremlins. I was worried about disappointing the publisher and getting terrible Amazon reviews. I was also making up my process as I went. I estimate writing my first book required five times as much energy as writing this one. Now I have a process that works for me, and I trust it.

Think about something you're great at. Now think about the first time you did it. You had potential, but you weren't that great — yet. You were creative, gutsy and driven, but you didn't have a process. Now you do that thing with both ease and excellence.

Part of maturing as a leader is developing processes and trusting them. Healthy leaders and organizations design processes for the big and little things. Building a process requires energy, but then our process can reproduce results. It's an investment that pays off later. It's great to be an amateur in something we love doing, but once we accept money for our work we're a professional. Are you acting like a pro? Do you have a process? Are you following it or winging it?

Building a process requires energy, but then our process can reproduce results.

My friend is an amazing fundraiser, an absolute pro. He raises millions of dollars a year for incredible causes and projects. How did he get so good? First of all, he's designed for it. He's got the raw materials to share vision and get people excited. Secondly, he spent years developing the necessary skills in other related fields that he transferred to his fundraising role. Third, he intentionally learns from some of the best fundraisers out there. Lastly, he has developed processes he repeats every year in order to see success. It's easy to view someone at the top of their field as a genius, but we didn't see the years of work they invested in their growth.

You can develop processes for almost anything, big or small.

Starting your day (I recommend Hal Elrod's *Miracle Morning* process)
Planning for your week (it's in our *Right Side up Journal*)
Completing a big project
Leading a meeting
Preparing to be gone for a week
Looking for a new job
Making a big purchase
Hiring a new team member
Writing a sales email
Setting your goals
Conducting an interview
Defining your boundaries

You may already have a process that's working, you just need to write it down. Formalizing a process in a visible document can skyrocket your productivity and multiply your impact. It's hard to repeat a process you haven't defined, but once you define it, you legitimize it. Then you can optimize it, and share it with others.

Every time I've defined a process, it has accelerated my work. After painfully wrestling my first book to the ground I had a developed a process I could repeat with future books. After a dozen people asked me, "What's your process for writing a book?" I finally wrote it down for others. Then I led a cohort to walk other writers through the process.

If you can't define your process, have others pull it out of you. It can be hard to see the process forest through the task of trees. If you can write your process on a napkin for your eight year old you're getting close. Once you have defined your process, you have to trust it. The next time that task comes up follow that process. The more you follow a process the less energy you'll burn thinking about it. Processes take the thinking out of challenging tasks. You can change your process later, but that's way easier than working from scratch.

The fear of a large deliverable never goes away, but the weight of the task can rest largely on the your process instead of on your shoulders.

> **Reflect on your processes**
>
> What task do I need to build a process for?
>
> What process could bring lightness to my team?
>
> Who can help me clarify or design these processes?

Imitate until you innovate

If I have seen further it is by standing on the shoulders of giants
Isaac Newton

I watch leaders shouldering a lot of weight by building everything themselves. They intentionally or unknowingly reject popular wisdom. Others have cheat codes that can speed you up and get you momentum faster. They've developed processes that have helped them succeed, and they're willing to give you these for free if you ask them right.

I love the spirit of innovation, but you can't innovate everything. Someone else has done the work you're doing . You can trail others who have figured things out. Ever hear the adage "Success leaves clues?" Imitation comes from wisdom. Even those launching a completely new product or a completely new concept can borrow from other fields.

I wanted to launch a new kind of coaching agency, and I wanted to be a different kind of coach. I tried to avoid being sales-y so much that I was weird when I talked about money. I lost opportunities. My sales pitch, or lack thereof, was confusing. My business strategy was *hard work + high quality + a spoonful of magic*. I tried many of my own ideas, and a few of them worked. The problem was I rejected tested methods to build a successful business. My friend had built a successful organization and had a combination of belief in me and pity on me. He taught me about marketing, client engagement, sales patterns and regular communication with clients. He pulled the light switch, lit up the room, became my business coach, and changed my life. Suddenly I had patterns to follow. The same tasks got easier, and I could put my best energy on serving my clients.

I am proud of our work at Stay Forth, and I believe we are a unique coaching agency. Finding proven processes for 80% of what we do has allowed us to create uniqueness in the other 20%. Now I get to train other coaches and help them skip years of pain that I experienced.

Imitate how others are succeeding, and eventually you can innovate new ways. What someone else has done may not be your final destination, but it can get you moving. Learn. Borrow. Repurpose. Repeat.

> **Reflect on imitating others**
>
> What skill do I need to learn?
>
> Who does this well?
>
> How can I borrow from their process?

Be accessible, not available

Distractions are plentiful. And time is short.
Adam Hochschild

One of the greatest challenges of being a leader is others seeking our attention. If you lead with excellence people will desire your time, decisions and inspiration. This has always been part of the leader gig, but the weight of this is immense today.

I don't think we realize how the pressure of being a leader has rapidly increased over the last few decades. The dark ages weren't that long ago. People used to have only three ways to reach leaders: find them in person, call them at work, or call them at home (if they were privy to your number). The higher on the organizational chart they were, the more their team guarded them. People would leave them a message with someone, and the leader could decide whether to call them back or not.

When email came on the scene, it promised to change the world. And it did. We had a great way to directly contact leaders at work on their massive desktop computers. Eventually they were able to check their rapidly expanding inbox on their desktop computer at home. Then laptops changed the game again. Work could happen at the office, at home, or at the coffee shop. Cell phones were also common, so people could go straight to the leader. There was no reason to call the office anymore.

The Blackberry, a hybrid between a phone and a computer, allowed leaders to shoot emails anytime, anywhere. Then, on January 9th, 2007, Steve Jobs made the famous announcement about the iPhone that changed the world. The communication boom exploded, and it's been expanding at light speed ever since.

Today the reachability of leaders is unbelievable. People have five or more ways to reach leaders directly (count them up). Most leaders are drowning in their communication outlets and expected to be readily available wherever they are. Leaders can work from anywhere and be reached everywhere. Yes, I admit to texting from the treadmill and the toilet. I'm not proud, just honest.

Here's the challenge: we must learn to limit our availability so we have enough space to create meaningful work and find margin away from work. This is not a problem to be solved; it's a tension to be managed. And it's only getting tougher. Communication constraints used to be external (others were guarding leaders' schedules), but now they are internal (we must guard our schedules). Leaders used to be barely reachable, now we are too reachable. Any leader set on resisting overwhelm and burnout must create boundaries for their communication outlets.

Cal Newport shares extensively about the challenge of producing good work in a digital age. He defines *deep work* as "Professional activities performed in a state of distraction-free concentration that push your cognitive capabilities to their limit. These efforts create new value, improve your skills, and are hard to replicate"[86]. Conversely, he defines *shallow work* as, "Non-cognitively demanding, logistical-style tasks, often performed while distracted. These efforts tend to not create much new value in the world and are easy to replicate"[87]. In a shallow world deep work is becoming increasingly valuable. Newport's hypothesis: "The ability to perform deep work is becoming increasingly rare at exactly the same time it is becoming increasingly valuable."[88] This means our attention is the asset we must guard. If you're being paid to lead you're also being paid to think deeply.

PART FOUR | Habits to keep you climbing

Creating things of meaning requires uninterrupted time and space to think deeply (those of you who work from home are nodding). Distractions and shallow work are always looming: the email you need to send, the task you need to check off, or the barrage of texts you're trying to catch up on. If we make ourselves available to everyone all the time our health, energy and impact will wane. We will cease creating meaningful things, abandon our priorities, feel our creativity flatten, and drift toward burnout.

But we can't swing the pendulum and stay tucked away in an ivory tower. Guarding our attention allows us to stay present to those we serve. Investing in our teams helps us cultivate three pillars: culture, conversation, and collaboration. People and tasks both matter, and we need a grid to do them both well. Every leader is pulled between people and projects. Leading people creates tension between uninterrupted solo time and collaborative team time.

The healthy leaders I interact with are constantly defining and holding communication boundaries. The unhealthy leaders I know are far too available. One leader I regularly interact with says he hates texting. He calls me randomly throughout the day, but I'm often with coaching clients and in focused meetings. After a few conversations educating him about my schedule, and plenty of missed calls, I texted him this reminder; "Due to my current coaching load, writing my next book, and family commitments, I have very few random slots open. You can get a hold of me or set up a meeting in the following ways… " Clear is kind, right? It's not fair to him to keep him guessing. It's my job to educate him and let him know how he can get my attention.

What's the difference between being available and being accessible?
An available leader can be interrupted by anyone in the moment.
An accessible leader can be reached by the appropriate people when needed.
An available leader responds to emails and texts constantly.
An accessible leader tackles email and texts when they can respond wisely.
An available leader regularly cancels meetings and delays personal projects.
An accessible leader guards crucial work blocks for projects and meetings.
An available leader allows interaction immediately.
An accessible leader creates space for interactions in appropriate timing.

223

See a pattern? There's a tyranny of the urgent that governs an available leader. Most leaders who become overly-available do so with good intentions. They want to stay connected with as many people as possible, but it simply isn't sustainable. Availability can stem from a fear of disappointing people, which, ironically, disappoints the people they care about the most. Overly-available leaders eventually devalue others. They pick up multiple calls during a meeting or cancel engagements because something "very important" came up (I guess I was unimportant?). I would rather someone tell me they do not have space to meet than cancel last minute or not be present when we meet.

> When we're confused about our commitments distractions are overwhelming, but when we're clear about our commitments distractions are manageable.

No one is perfect here, exceptions and emergencies come up. Don't beat yourself up, but do make a communication plan. When we pre-decide on communication, our communication decisions get easier. When are you available for calls? When do you answer texts and emails? Who can interrupt you? What constitutes an emergency? If you decide on these ahead of time you can move from reactive communication to proactive communication. Like any process it takes time to learn, but pays off later.

I'm not advocating for being unreachable or ghosting people. I'm advocating for protecting and cultivating the relationships and commitments that matter most to you. You didn't promise to answer a random sales email, but you do have commitments to your team.

When we're confused about our commitments distractions are overwhelming, but when we're clear about our commitments distractions are manageable. We have to clarify our commitments if we're going to protect them. When you're available to your highest priority relationships you won't have space for everyone. After I write these words I have two crucial coaching sessions where I will be fully focused on those teams followed by three family commitments where I will be fully focused on my family. If I try to cram a few more things into my day I will break my commitments to all of them. The inbox and task list will have to wait until Monday.

When we become available to everyone, we'll neglect those we love most and ourselves. Neglecting our needs shows up in areas like nutrition (or eating altogether), sleep, margin, exercise, and rest. Just because you could make time for others doesn't mean you need to pick up the phone or jump into your inbox. You can schedule an email block or a phone call for tomorrow or next week.

Every call, email or text looks urgent; our brains don't know the difference at first. *Do Not Disturb* and *Airplane Mode* are your buddies. You must pre-make these decisions through processes or you will fall to your impulses in the moment. A telemarketer does not deserve the same attention as my son.

In-person boundaries can be just as challenging as communication outlets. Perhaps your company has had an open door policy for years, but this brings you forty interruptions a day, leaving you constantly behind on your projects. You start to believe, "in order to get through my emails and get my projects done I have to get in super early, or stay late." Create an alternative, and communicate it clearly to the team. Many teams have moved to hybrid schedules like three days in the office and two remote days in order to separate people time and project time.

I love training teams and speaking to groups, but I've had to create boundaries around this. After speaking to groups, people want to talk to you. Sometimes I have a commitment (like getting to the airport), or I know I'll be exhausted and need to recover. Before I get on a stage, I decide whether I'll be available after the talk to chat with folks, and I tell them. Sometimes people ask, "Do you have a few minutes to chat?" It's never JUST a few minutes. I'll often say, "I don't have time to chat, but do you have a specific question?" Sometimes they do and I say, "You can email me, and I will send you a resource." I've found people driven enough to follow up with an email are usually the people I like to help. And you don't owe anything to the ones who never follow up.

This may seem cold. Perhaps you feel like it's overkill. Maybe you aren't having issues managing your influence, but I guarantee you the more you lead with excellence the more people will want your time. Don't wait until you're overloaded to make the shift from available to accessible. Trading availability for accessibility allows you to order your priorities. You will disappoint plenty of people as a human and especially as a leader. The trick is making sure you don't disappoint your highest priority relationships. The email can wait until Monday, but my daughter's concert will start on time with or without me.

> **Reflect on your accessibility and availability**
>
> How clear are my boundaries for my communication channels? (1-10)
>
> How well am I prioritizing my commitments in this season? (1-10)
>
> What one change do I need to make to my accessibility?

Stop adding value; multiply it

Everybody can be great because everybody can serve.
Martin Luther King, Jr

As I've studied incredible leaders at a distance and coach them up close I've noticed something unique about the greats. They don't add value, they multiply it. They know their purpose, and dedicate much of their time to serving others. They've learned what they're great at and how to leverage that skill or gift. They've shifted from an addition mindset to a multiplication mindset.

Multiplying allows leaders to bypass burnout while making a serious impact over the long haul. Maybe you've been adding for years, and you're wondering why you feel stuck. Multiplication thinking can unlock new levels of impact with far less energy.

Perhaps the easiest example is how we spread our ideas. Addition thinking could be selling, training and educating others one-on-one. You may be focusing on individuals instead of groups. It's tiring, discouraging and requires a lot of energy to say the same thing over and over again. I know, because I used to operate this way.

Make a way to let your ideas spread. If you can create something once and use it many times, you'll lessen the weight of your work while increasing your impact. By simply transferring your ideas into a visual, a tool, or a process, you can increase the reach. Once you've created them, they can multiply for you. Technology allows us to multiply messages easily from webinars to podcasts to group meetups to slack to group emails. People can be multipliers, also. Ideas get multiplied through teams and catalysts who can spread your message to many others. The internet brings people and technology together, which makes it an ideal multiplier (for good and for ill).

> Multiplication thinking can turn impact for one into impact for many.

Concepts I share on *Stay Forth Leadership Podcast* episodes often come to me during one-on-one coaching sessions. I hone them and ensure they will provide value to many more people. It takes roughly an hour to prepare for and record an episode. Then my teammate, Jonathan, edits them and releases them on Thursdays to thousands of people. Not only do people listen to them that week, but I often share episodes later with folks seeking clarity on that specific concept instead of repeating it to them.

Multiplication thinking can turn impact for one into impact for many. If you can create something once and it helps you or others many times over, that's multiplication. Addition yields linear results, but multiplication yields residual results.[89] If you continue adding, you will limit your impact and increase your risk of burnout.

I'm not asking you to lose focus on individuals and launch everything on a mega level. Even if you were to expose your idea to five people at a time instead of one that's 5x multiplication. Multiplication thinking can help prepare people before meetings and call them to action after meetings. Most people study you and your organization online before they meet with you. If you give meaningful pathways for them to learn beforehand, your time with them can be more valuable. You can send your potential client a podcast, tool, pitch, or intro video ahead of time and have a running start for your meeting.

PART FOUR | Habits to keep you climbing

Here is a five step process to multiply yourself and your ideas.

Name what you want more of. Multiplying anything starts with naming want you want to produce more of. Get specific. *What are you trying to get more of? Why?*

Give yourself permission to create it. In order to invest precious time into developing that thing you must give yourself permission to invest in it. You have to believe it will matter to others, or you'll push it aside. It's helpful to get accountability from others. *What are you going to develop? How will this impact people?*

Release it to the world. At some point you need to hit publish and share it with others. You can do this in small ways like emailing it to a small group or sharing with a test group or large ways like mass email or a marketing campaign. Aim for an effective launch over a big launch. *When will you release this? Who are you aiming at? What channels will you release it through?*

Practice the craft regularly. If it was helpful to produce this once, it can be much more helpful to produce this regularly. Your practice will increase your excellence. You will get better over time. If the first event, episode, article, course, meeting, or group email was helpful make space to do that regularly. Make sure you're "practicing in public" so your ideas can impact others, you can gather feedback, and you can make changes. *What is your process to share this with others and refine it?*

Leverage it for the greatest possible impact. Once you are regularly producing your resource, you can leverage it for more impact. A lever gives mechanical advantage that makes you more productive with less energy. Leveraging multiplies the impact as much as possible. Once it's out in the world, you can bolster the reach by sharing in new channels, developing partnerships, or connecting it with your other offerings. *How can you leverage this for the greatest possible impact over time? What people and channels can help you extend the reach?*

Reflect on multiplying

In what specific way/s do I need to multiply instead of adding?

If my impact multiplies how will people be better off?

What is my next step toward multiplication?

Stay (constantly) aware of your season

There is a time for everything,
and a season for every activity under the heavens
King Solomon

Many years ago a friend told me, "I'm in a busy season. Things will slow down here soon." He was running hard in his business, his kids needed his focus, and he served on a board that required a big commitment. Each time I saw him over the next several years, he said the same thing; "I'm in a busy season. Things will slow down here soon". Fifteen years later he is saying a similar thing. For my friend, this is not a season; this is his life. His mindset has impacted his family, his health, his relationships, and his business. Be careful hiding behind the word "season" as an excuse to stay stuck in old ways because you're avoiding change.

The weather has seasons. Life also has seasons. When we understand the season we're in, we can match it with appropriate actions. I call this "seasonal awareness." Winter has different challenges and opportunities than summer.

We approach life differently in different seasons. In the summer, I work short days so I can get outside with my kids. During the holiday season, our family has ongoing activities, but we know the week after

AntiBurnout

Christmas is a week to relax, watch family movies, and prepare for the next year. The fall ushers in beautiful moments to go to the mountains in flannels peeping the yellow aspens.

> Awareness of the season we're in gives us awareness of the actions we should be taking.

Leadership has seasons, too. The startup season can be incredibly taxing. Many times these startup tasks are outside of a leader's passion zone. Money is often razor thin, and it's hard to justify paying others to do the work. There's an ongoing list of things to do: from bank accounts to legal work to articles of incorporation to finding professionals to help with all the nuanced tasks. It's helpful for leaders in a startup season to remember it won't always be this way. It can't always be this way. It's okay to run hard for a time when we know there's an actual light at the end of the tunnel. At the end of the startup season it's crucial to define what season is next and what it will require.

After a fun, but stressful infancy season, our small team at Stay Forth needed to discover new ways to reach new markets and serve new types of leaders. COVID-19 season had worn many organizations down, and many were hesitant to spend money. I discerned it was time to enter an *experimentation* season. I was clear with my team: "many of our experiments won't work. Failing will be defined as not trying new things." We launched new programs, took calculated risks, and I launched a new program combining several coaching processes. We discovered which things rose to the surface and which ones sunk. That season was thrilling. And stressful. But all seasons come to an end. We knew it was time to enter a new season; *focus*.

During the *focus* season, we eliminated anything that wasn't bringing huge return on energy (ROE). We committed to leveraging a few things for the greatest impact. Those things grew, which led to our next season; *expansion*. We had enough bandwidth to add a few things again. *Experimentation* season revealed what was worth investing in, and *focus* season revealed what could be expanded on. When you know the season of your leadership or organization you can commit to timely actions without **committing to them forever.**

Awareness of the season we're in gives us awareness of the actions we should be taking. I don't know how to reevaluate the season without space and reflection. It requires distancing yourself enough to look back and look ahead. Ron Heifetz refers to this process of objective evaluation as moving from the dance floor to the balcony.[90] When we're making moves on the floor, it's hard to get a true picture of what's going on around us. When we're aware of the season we're in and the season that is coming, we can make the necessary moves.

> **Reflect on your season**
>
> What season have you come from?
>
> What season do you believe you are in or heading into?
>
> What activities should you say YES to in this season?
>
> What activities should you say NO to in this season?

Utilize rest and momentum to your advantage

Creating momentum is like launching a rocket. You'll use a disproportionate amount of energy to get off the ground, but once you overcome gravity, you can maintain your momentum with minimal effort.
Craig Groeschel

I was sitting atop the cliffs on a perfect day in Santa Cruz, California. At a distance I could see a pack of surfers hanging out on their boards resting and chatting it up. They waited several minutes for a set to come in. As it approached, they dropped to their chests ready to catch the next wave. They passed on good waves. It was clear they were waiting for "the big one."

Suddenly they dropped on their chests, looked back over their shoulder and took six hard strokes. This gave them enough momentum to catch the wave, hop to their feet, and ride it close to cliffs whooping and hollering. It was art in motion. They repeated this process for the next few hours making it look easy. They were working with the energy of the waves. Whenever I surf I make it look really hard, and I find myself working against the waves. I end up calling it quits from pure exhaustion after paddling constantly. I don't seem to catch as many waves as the locals next to me.

Wise leaders utilize rest and momentum to their advantage. They see leadership in seasons that require resting, working hard, and experiencing thrilling forward momentum from time to time. Wise leaders learn to work with the flow of the season, not against it. Let's take a look at these different seasons of leadership with our surfer friends in mind.

A rest season: relaxing on their surfboard. This is a period of time where a leader or a team intentionally lives under their capacity. They understand they can pull up and get a bit of rest from exertion between sets. It may be a sabbatical, but more likely it is a time of preparation to store up energy for later. The right season for rest varies with the industry or the organization, but it only happens through intention and proactivity.

A bust season: paddling to get into the big wave. This is a period of time where a leader or team pushes hard. Like the surfer paddling hard to get into the wave there is a definite purpose behind their paddling. They may have to paddle hard multiple times to get into their next opportunity. They dig deep, stay focused, show some grit and trust the ride will be worth it.

A thrust season: catching the wave. This is a period of time where a leader or team experiences momentum. After hard, measured work, the team or organization experiences something greater than they could summon themselves. It's thrilling to feel the momentum from the launch, growth, increased revenue or life transformation. This thrust can launch them into new challenges, like a surfer being caught below the wave or heading toward the rocks. Amidst the thrill, new challenges and issues arise.

A rust season: swimming to shore prematurely. This is what results when a leader or team runs out of energy. Everyone else is having a great time catching waves, and they have nothing left in the tank. They paddle to shore and cash it in early. This is what burnout feels like. It requires extended rest out of the waves in order to recover. Eventually it requires a fundamentally different way to function so it doesn't happen again. When the waves of life and leadership are

PART FOUR | Habits to keep you climbing

quickly approaching a leader it's easy to over-exert and rust out. These seasons can sneak up on leaders. It's a terrible feeling.

A surfer has to carefully select the waves they're going to bet on. The one they let pass gives way to the big one. Carefully choosing our opportunities is vital to living and leading whelmed. Sometimes we decide to bust our butts to capitalize on the opportunity and other times we rest up for the next wave that will give us an incredible ride.

Thrust seasons require paddling out to the right spot, resting, and busting our butts to get into the big wave. Many leaders and organizations want thrust without having to bust, and that's just not possible. The private work of learning and training comes out when they're riding the wave.

The magical force called momentum
There's nothing like the magical force called momentum. When we have it things move smoother, easier and faster. It feels like an unfair advantage, and it is. It's hard to generate, but once you have it things get rolling. Momentum can produce results in moments that would otherwise take years.

In his classic book *Good to Great*, organizational thinker and business consultant Jim Collins, describes a concept called "the flywheel effect." Imagine a large wooden wheel. As you grab the worn wooden pegs it feels nearly impossible to get moving, but after some serious effort it starts spinning. Once you get some momentum it feels nearly impossible to stop. Remember Newton's Law of Inertia from science class? *An object at rest stays at rest and an object in motion stays in motion unless acted on by an outside force.* The smallest bit of inertia can get you and your team moving faster. Focus and force transfer potential energy into actual energy (kinetic energy).

When the project feels hard at first, don't worry; this is normal. It's a law of nature. Momentum is often the result of careful preparation and intentional steps. When we've been working, learning, preparing or thinking in a focused direction the next step often presents itself quickly. This book feels like a flywheel. I've been developing these ideas, principles, and tools and coaching them into leaders and teams for over a decade. Synthesizing them was a lot easier than creating them, because I already had momentum.

> Don't wait on momentum to magically happen; take steps to generate it. Start where you are. Take small steps. Get the flywheel moving.

Momentum is exponentially helpful in leadership. A plane burns a lot of fuel in takeoff. So do projects and organizations. If we have some momentum before takeoff, we can catch some lift. Great leaders work with momentum; most leaders work against it. As you stare that next project in the eyes, and your pits begin to sweat remember you've already done some of the work. I bet you're not starting from zero. I bet the wheel is already moving.

Many people never accomplish their big dreams, because they're passively waiting for something to magically present itself. They're waiting for permission, funding, a team, a chunk of time or the day they feel smart enough. Most people get stuck before they get started. If you're waiting for those things to magically present themselves you'll be waiting a long time. Start getting momentum now.

When we think like a victim, we stay stuck. But when we think like a designer, we build our way forward. It may feel hard at first, but if it's worth taking on the big dream it's worth getting started on now. Don't wait on momentum to magically happen; take steps to generate it. Start where you are. Take small steps. Get the flywheel moving.

Write the talk two weeks before you have to.
Lay out your clothes the night before your big meeting.
Make five sales calls.
Finish the presentation a week ahead of time and get some feedback from your team.
Get to bed early the night before that gathering you're hosting.
Schedule the appointment with a trainer at the gym.
Start waking up early.
Create the pitch deck.

PART FOUR | Habits to keep you climbing

Sketch out the job description for your next hire.
Read five pages.
Create the agenda for next staff meeting, and send it out early.
Let your direct report know the issue you'd like to address ahead of time.
Make that dinner reservation.

> **Reflect on momentum**
>
> What waves of momentum can I ride personally or professionally?
>
> What are a few upcoming rest breaks I can take?
>
> How can I start creating momentum now toward my big dream?

Show your work

Great communication begins with connection
Oprah Winfrey

M ath was not kind to me in school. I still don't know how to solve the "train leaves Chicago at 3:00 and DesMoines at 3:45" problems. I had one bully more terrifying than the rest; Algebra. I still shudder when I say the word. I spent at least half of my energy my freshman year of high school on algebra alone. My Algebra teacher, Mrs. Conrod, gave me a hack: "If you show your work on a problem, and get the answer wrong, I'll give you half credit." Right process + Wrong answer = 50%. That allowed me to pass Algebra.

I've observed the same principle to be true for leaders; when we get the wrong answer, but we show others our process they are likely to give us half credit. When you show others the process behind your work, people can track with you. I call this process of showing your work "communicating from context with clarity". Every leader is a communicator. The question is not, "Will you communicate?" but "Will you communicate effectively?"

Reasonable people will give you the benefit of the doubt. And it's not worth reasoning with unreasonable people, anyway. Showing your work by slowing down to communicate clearly will require more energy, but delivers better results.

> Clear communication requires energy in the present but limits confusion and conflict in the future.

I experienced this firsthand when I had to make a hard directional move at Stay Forth. After much wrestling, we decided we would no longer have an in-house coaching network. The easiest and fastest thing to do would've been sending a group email and moving on. But that wouldn't show them dignity or give them a chance to understand why we made this decision. I dreaded having to call every one of our coaches and tell them the news.

I called each person except one (she had no desire to hear my reasoning). I clearly explained the last two years of context, owned a few mistakes, bluntly shared the decision we had come to, and gave them space for questions. They were appreciative. A few of them even expressed relief, and thanked me for the conversation. I'm glad I did it this way, but it was exhausting.

Sharing the context of a decision gives people a chance to track with the decision instead of just reacting to it. I've watched leaders change a whole team's decision when they showed their work. One leader changed a group recommendation by sharing just ten minutes of context.

Communicating from context

Part of the role of a leader is making decisions. It's weighty, and can be tiring ("decision fatigue" is real!). Sometimes we can share the context of the decision before it's made, and other times we have to share after the decision is made. When a leader shares the context of a decision, they have a greater chance of creating alignment on the team.

Here are a few ways you can start with "why" in your communication.
Why we value these things here in our team or organization
Why this decision should be made now
Why I'm leaning this way or why we made this decision

Why I'm moving forward quickly or slowing the process down
Why I made the decision I did
Here are some ways you can start with "how" in your communication.
How I/we went about this process
How this will impact the team or organization
How this can create a better future

Educating others on the context behind our decision can increase trust and limit criticism. Even if they disagree with your decision, they may give you half credit for your process. Some will not, but they have already closed their mind. Some will be glad you invited them into the process, and can add value along the way. Others will just need time to process this and will come around later.

Communicating with clarity
When the time is right, share the decision clearly. Don't beat around the bush, don't lie and don't manipulate. People can smell the stench of B.S., and it's not dignifying. Remember, clear is kind.

I promise you this, you don't communicate as clearly as you think. People can't read your mind. I have accidentally hurt people and slowed down projects by being unclear about decisions or expectations. Be ridiculously clear.

Sometimes it's not you, it's them. When humans are emotionally elevated, distracted or tired we activate our monkey brain. We aren't able to take in the message, and we hear only what we want to hear or have space to hear. Have you ever been gravely misconstrued? *"How could they get THAT conclusion from our conversation?!?"* Misconstrued communication may not be your fault, but it's your responsibility. If you're coming into a crucial meeting with a specific message to communicate write it down ahead of time, say it word for word, and follow up your conversation in writing.

There are several reasons clear communication is especially vital right now.

Speed is high. We're moving so fast we rarely slow down to communicate well.

Change is high. When a lot is changing our process can create safety.

Criticism is high. While we can never please everyone, it's vital to give others the chance to understand our thought process in a calm, rational manner. These divisive times have conditioned us to fight instead of listening.

Desire for collaboration is high. People want to shape outcomes with others; not simply have decisions handed to them.

Communicating from context with clarity can yield the following results.

Gives a greater chance for wisdom, alignment, and buy-in
Diffuses future conflict
Allows others to follow the process logically instead of reacting emotionally
Creates psychological safety for our team
Deepens trust in us, our team or our organization.

I know this requires more energy than making quick decisions, but I promise it's a lighter way to lead. Clear communication requires energy in the present but limits confusion and conflict in the future. Invest energy now, and it will require less later. Every leader is a communicator. Wise leaders communicate from context with clarity.

> **Reflect on clear communication**
>
> In what situations do I move too quickly in my communication?
>
> What are the effects?
>
> If I asked my team, "when do you wish I communicated more clearly" what would they say?

PART FIVE
Essentials for the long climb

PART FIVE | Essentials for the long climb

The smallest essentials can bring the greatest returns.

Those who discover greatness seem to have an ability to connect the biggest things in life with the smallest things. Anyone can string together a great year, but few live a great life. Most people do annual goal planning, but few zoom out to do life planning. If careers, decades and dreams matter, so do Tuesday afternoons and Saturday mornings. The little things are the pathway to the big ones.

Your vision for the good life is different than mine, but I hope this book has helped you to get a clear vision for your life and leadership.

> If you want a lighter way to lead; think longer.

There is a lighter path in this heavy world. It's possible to live and lead for the long haul without burning out or losing your soul in the process. Jesus of Nazareth cast a vision for a lighter burden, and I'm crazy enough to believe it's possible. I want to serve people, maximize my potential and elevate others for as long as I can. What about you?

It's easy to get knocked off course on our climb. I've watched the same bullies come steal energy from leaders. I've also seen healthy leaders cover these foundations and tap into regular wells of energy. If you want a lighter way to lead; think longer. If you can understand what you need in these foundational areas, you can get the flywheel of your energy turning smoothly and regularly. I keep an eye on these. If you can identify a gap or an issue you can take steps to replenish your energy. Remember, clarity should always move us to courage.

I approach leadership from a practical viewpoint, not a scientific one. I'm not a doctor, psychologist, or a therapist. You may have an area out of whack below the surface that is a serious issue requiring professional help. If you have ongoing concerns in any of these areas, start by consulting a physician.

AntiBurnout

The essential of sleep

Our culture under-values sleep, but adequate sleep is vital to showing up well for others.

Leaders often believe they must sacrifice sleep for impact. This belief can be rooted in feeling behind, over-functioning for others or procrastination. Under-valuing sleep will wear us down and impact other areas of our life and leadership. Many of the best leaders are dogmatic about their sleep schedule and even their naps.

What do I need to do in order to maximize my sleep?

How many hours of sleep do I need to be sharp and well-rested?

The essential of routine

Leaders must understand their personal and family needs and prioritize them regularly.

Leaders should expect to be pulled in different directions by requests and expectations. A healthy routine may shift during the year, but a wise leader creates a daily and weekly routine that keeps them healthy and effective. A healthy life is much bigger than being effective at work.

What necessities should be in my daily routine? My weekly routine?

How can I maximize my daily and weekly routine?

The essential of spiritual connection

Leaders with an ongoing spiritual connection find deeper meaning, and often, greater longevity in their work.

A spiritual connection reminds us that life is bigger than ourselves, and not everything rests on us. Research is clear that in order to make meaning, we must engage with something larger than ourselves.[91] A spiritual basis for our work gives us purpose and allows us to view ourselves as stewards of our role and our influence, instead of drivers. It can also allow us to differentiate our identity (who we are) from our impact (what we do). At the end of the best, or worst, day I know I am beloved because I am a child of God, not because I perform. It takes the pressure off.

What is the foundation below my work?

What beliefs keep me going when I'm tired or dispassionate?

The essential of exercise

Exercise is a maximizer that can feed every area of life and leadership.

Every person has different exercise needs and challenges. While leaders may feel tired and mentally taxed, exercise is a great investment to fight for. Exercise often distracts a leader creating separation from "work brain" and fresh ideas. Movement creates energy. It's an investment that pays great returns.

What's the right exercise plan for me?

When will I schedule exercise into my life?

The essential of work boundaries

Most leaders are working from a place of depletion, not replenishment, which is eroding their productivity and effectiveness.

If we do not clearly define our work hours our lives become a swamp of work-like activities. Many leaders are not getting adequate recovery time for their brains and bodies. A lack of margin slowly erodes creativity, sharpness and meaning from work.

What boundaries do I need to put around my work time?

What activities are helpful for me to replenish my energy each day and week?

The essential of limiting caffeine and adrenaline

Many leaders over-rely on caffeine and adrenaline delivering a false high, which eventually results in depletion or a crash.

When we depend on caffeine and adrenaline, this gives a false sense of energy. Both of these can mask our foundational needs. Eventually they both wear off and can create long-term effects on our health. When we live and lead rushed, we live in fight or flight mode and call on adrenaline to sustain us. This is particularly dangerous, because it's hard to measure or even realize we are abusing this natural chemical.[92]

What is the appropriate amount of caffeine for me?

What would my spouse or friends say about the pace of my life and leadership?

The essential of a healthy diet

Leaders must work to find the rhythm and role of food in their life.

Food is a catalyst area. When we're eating poorly other disciplines dissipate. When we're eating well, other disciplines rise. When we live reactively we rarely think about the food we consume. Nourishing foods can bring us greater energy and set us up for long-term health. It's a battle to eat well, but one worth fighting in order to live and lead well.

What changes do I need to make to my food intake?

How proactive am I about the food I consume each day? (1-10)

The essential of limiting technology

Technology can work for or against a leader, creating massive advantages and massive distractions.

Technology is a great tool and a terrible master. Great leaders leverage the power of technology and create boundaries around the distractions. Leaders must constantly reassess technology's effects and opportunities. Over-indulgence in our screens, information flow and email increases decision fatigue and limits replenishment.

How can I more effectively leverage technology?

In what areas do I need to limit my technology usage?

The essential of relational connection

Great leaders seek to lead inter-dependently, not independently.

We cannot do meaningful work long-term in isolation. We are built for connection from the moment of conception. We are relational beings, yet many times we believe we can lead great things alone. Wise leaders lead from among a community they are inter-dependently connected to. Connection brings meaning to life and work, and multiples our creativity.

How connected am I to those in my team and organization? (1-10)

In what specific ways could increasing my connection increase my health or impact?

PART SIX
Practices for the climb

The little stuff we do repeatedly catalyzes health and impact.

The rigors of life and the challenge of the leadership climb can wear us down. It's hard enough to keep our pace on the climb. We don't need extra weight in our packs. Small practices help us continue elevating over time. These practices transform into sacred rituals. Greg McKeown calls rituals "habits with a soul."[93]

The little stuff compounds. These "atomic habits."[94] bring tiny gains in the short-term, but have deep impact over time. Sometimes we experiment and trip over something great. Here are some ideas that work for different leaders I respect. You may choose to experiment with them or implement them into your routine. Learn from them and try them, but you'll have to customize them for you.

Recovery practices

Any elite athlete knows recovery is vital to the body's performance. Recovery rhythms separate the high performers from the highest performers. At the apex of any field, the difference in skills is so small that recovery is the greatest way to establish a gap. We've been so focused on leadership development we've forgotten about leadership recovery. Alex Soojung-Kim Pang says, "Rest, it turns out, is not work's competitor; it is work's partner."[95] Margin can create movement. The ones who keep climbing for the long haul discover and practice rhythms of recovery.

Create an "end of workday ritual" and stick to it
Discover a hobby that brings you delight
Sleep in once or twice a week
Practice a weekly sabbath where you produce nothing
Leave your laptop at the office (or give it to your spouse to hide it)
Put your phone to bed in another room at 8PM
Neglect your email on the weekends
Find a nap rhythm that works for you
Dedicate vacations as "No work zones"
Learn and practice breathing work

Physical health practices

Many leaders function like brains on a stick. Our bodies are more than just carriers for our mind; they are essential elements to a life of vitality. When we're young we can get away with mistreating our bodies, but it catches up with us eventually. Investing in practices for a healthy body stimulates our minds, creates a quality of life, allows us to be present with those we love, and paves a path for a long life.

Walk a mile a day
Schedule your exercise
Drink a full bottle of water first thing (even before coffee)
Plan your meals the night before
Get adequate sleep
Decide on and stick to your caffeine limit
Lay out your gym bag the night before
Discover ways to make your workout fun (or give yourself a reward afterward)
Treat yourself to silence or a stimulating audio book when you work out
Invest in a massage occasionally

Mental health practices

We're living through a mental health epidemic. Our brains are perpetually overstimulated. Everyone is fighting for our best attention. Healthy humans and leaders will have to constantly fight for brain-space and mental health. Mental exhaustion is always a few steps away. But so is mental clarity. Creativity and empathy require mental space.

Look back at your day and week to identify wins
Get outside to be still and to move
Take occasional social media breaks or quit social media
Designate times for no emails, calls and texts
Create a stop time for work each day
Create a "to don't" list each week
Develop a consistent bedtime and rise time
Wait an hour or two into your day to answer texts or emails
Take five minute rest breaks in the sun between meetings
Take short naps occasionally (20-35 minutes is optimal)

PART SIX | Practices for the climb

Emotional health practices

It's important for leaders to stay emotionally stable. Especially parents! As the adage goes; "When emotions are high intelligence is low." Emotions are a beautiful part of our design, but they can hijack our decisions if we're not careful. When we spin out of control, our family, friends, and teams will feel it, too. But when we remain grounded, we cultivate an environment of connection and alignment.

Journal what you're feeling occasionally (Thursdays in the Right Side up Journal)
Read a book just for fun (with no benefit to your work)
Plan your day and week ahead of time
Read for ten minutes before bed
Pray daily
Tell your team when you won't respond to texts or emails
Create and stick to a sabbath weekly
Invest in a few sessions with a therapist and see what it unlocks
Dial in a daily routine
Block off a half day monthly or quarterly to create whatever you want
Change up your work location occasionally
Name the gap between your expectations and reality
Find a friend you can be honest with
Reflect on a few beautiful moments you experienced during that week

Vocational health practices

Work can be a huge source of fulfillment and a huge source of stress. Your work is not synonymous with your career. It's so much deeper than that. You have sacred work to do in various areas of life from your family to your community to your volunteerism to your church to your clients. Keeping a proper perspective of the sacred work you've been invited into is vital for meaning and longevity.

Read a testimonial of your work or encouraging note occasionally
Revisit your WHY often
Rehash a failure that created a victory
Invest in coaching
Find a way to celebrate when goals are achieved

Volunteer regularly for an organization or cause you care about
Help your kids start a business
Ask yourself, "What do I hope results from this activity?"
Give a percentage of your profits away
Create a grid for saying yes and no to requests
Use all your allotted vacation days
Reevaluate which meetings can be eliminated or cut in half (quarterly)

Relational health practices

Relationships are the good stuff in life. They are the things that truly matter and the things that last after retirement. I've never met an elderly person who looked back at their life and regretted over-investing in people or being too active in their community. Have you? But retirement homes are full of people wishing they had invested more in those they loved. Maybe you've heard the haunting truth, "The only ones who will remember if you worked late ten years from now are your kids." We need more leaders who clearly prioritize relationships over their work.

Come home early occasionally
Write encouraging notes regularly
Thank people when they do something for you (texting videos is my favorite)
Check in with friends randomly (calls, voice memos or video apps)
Take a walk with a friend, coworker, your spouse or your kids
Write down 3 "pocket questions" you can pull out at any moment
Share "highs and lows" with your family or team
Develop a hobby you can do with friends
Create a "phone a friend" buddy who can help you make hard decisions
Reconnect with one old friend for a call weekly

CONCLUSION
The old man & the hourglass

As I write this I'm looking up from my desk at two mementos: a note and an hourglass. The hourglass is framed by golden rods and mounted on two beautiful birchwood squares. Sand is slipping through the small gap in the glass. It reminds me time is precious, and our days aren't guaranteed. It challenges me to seize moments to invest in the people I love. It invites me to live each moment with intention.

The note sits open on my desk. It's penned in shaky handwriting, and its author has experienced a long, full life. The words are sincere and laced with care for me and my family. The old man writes encouraging notes to my family and I each month. I always smile as I pause to read them.

That old an is my grandfather. At the time this book was released he was ninety seven. He and my Grandma traveled the world together before she passed away. He went sky diving for the first time at ninety, and he still has a few big trips planned. He isn't just my Grandpa; he is a model of the ideals I want to live by.

He doesn't have much time left in his hourglass. Sometimes I pause to think about the words I will say at his memorial, whether that is next month or four years from now. When I step up the podium I'll share stories of things he did that other old men simply don't do. I have fond memories of this church; it's the same place I shared stories of my Grandma and watched my Grandpa exchange vows from a wheelchair to his next wife. I'll share these words about his life.

He lived every day as an adventure.
He treated you like you were the only one in the room.
He did stuff that others only talked about.
He lived fully right to the end.

Each one of us gets to decide what truly matters to us. Once we do it's our responsibility to live toward those things. Let's take our gaze off what others are doing and do the work to design this one life we've been given.

What is it you plan to do with your one wild and precious life?
Poet Mary Oliver

Recommended resources to go deeper

The aim of this book was to give you a practical plan for living and leading healthy for the long haul. I've touched on many topics that might require a much deeper dive for you. Here is a list of books I highly recommend if you want to go deeper on any of the following topics.

Leading with vulnerability and authenticity: *Dare to Lead* and *Braving the Wilderness* by Brené Brown

Building a healthy organization: *The Advantage* by Patrick Lencioni

Leadership as design: *Designing your life* by Bill Burnett and Dave Evans, *Change by Design* by Tim Brown

Investing in others: *Multipliers* by Liz Wiseman

Boundaries: *Boundaries for Leaders* by Henry Cloud

Shortening your work week: *Shorter* by Alex Soojung-Kim Pang

Simplifying your life: *Essentialism* by Greg McKeown

Understanding your wiring: *The Six Types of Working Genius* by Patrick Lencioni

Becoming a creative professional: Any books by Austin Kleon, *Going Pro* and *The War of Art* by Steven Pressfield, *The accidental Creative* by Todd Henry

Rest and replenishment: *Sacred Rest* by Saundra Dalton Smith

Marketing and storytelling: B*uilding a Story Brand* by Donald Miller

Focusing your mind: *Mindshift* by Erwin McManus, *Deep Work* and *Digital Minimalism* by Cal Newport

The effects of adrenaline: *The Hidden Link Between Adrenaline and Stress* by Archibald Hart

Leading at the Executive level: *The Effective Executive* by Peter Drucker, *Good to Great* by Jim Collins

Burnout (with a focus on women): *Burnout* by Emily and Amelia Nagoski

Notes

About the author

Alan Briggs loves outdoor adventures in the Colorado high country, but the greatest adventure of his life is being a husband to Julie and a dad to his four kids.

He helps catalytic leaders leverage catalytic moments for systemic change. He partners to create transformation through coaching leaders and teams, speaking to groups and training teams. Alan also curates a hub for connection, collaboration and coworking in Colorado Springs.

He designed the the *Right Side up Journal* as a daily companion for leaders who want to get healthy and reach sustainable impact. You can follow his curiosity and fresh content by listening to Stay Forth Leadership Podcast.

Invite Alan to invest in you or your team

Alan and the team at Stay Forth serve leaders through one-on-one leadership coaching, leadership cohorts, sabbatical coaching, speaking to teams and groups, consulting with organizations and hosting leadership experiences in Colorado.

To inquire about Alan serving you or your team please fill out this form

More ways to grow with Stay Forth

JOIN AN EFFECTIVE LEADER COHORT

We believe in developing leadership skills, not taking leadership pills. We host cohorts 3-5 times a year to help leaders and teams grow in their awareness (new information) and action (new steps). Leaders take an assessment to gauge their obstacles and opportunities then they learn the "8 core skills of effective leadership" over eight weeks in a caring community.

ORDER A RIGHT SIDE UP JOURNAL FOR YOU AND YOUR TEAM!

We hope you have grown daily through utilizing this paper version of the journal. We also have an optimized digital version of this journal.

LISTEN TO STAY FORTH LEADERSHIP PODCAST

Leadership is challenging, a lot like climbing a mountain. The Stay Forth Leadership Podcast is a resource to help you become an effective leader- someone who is healthy, self-aware, and working with the grain of their gifting at a sustainable pace to produce long-term impact. Each week, Alan Briggs hosts practical conversations with leadership experts designed to equip you with tools to produce the highest amount of change possible through new awareness, new information, new tools, and processes to guide you on your journey to become the healthiest and most impactful leader you can be.

Additional tools to guide your journey.

QUARTERLY ENERGY MAP

Plan out the energy required for the next 3 months.

Scan to download the　　　　　Scan for tips on
Quarterly Energy Map　　　　 using this tool

WHEEL OF TRANSFORMATION

*Walk through a progression from
CONFUSION to CLARITY to COURAGE to CONSISTENCY.*

Scan to download the　　　　　Scan for tips on
Wheel of Transformation　　　 using this tool

UNIQUE DESIGN FRAMEWORK

Clarify your wiring and how you best live this out.

Scan to download the　　　　　Scan for tips on
Unique Design Framework　　　using this tool

Endnotes

PART ONE

1. Brown, Brené, Braving the Wilderness, NY, Penguin Random House, 2017, 10.
2. Soojung-Kim Pang, Alex, Shorter, NY, Hachette Book Group, 2020, 20.
3. Han, Byung-Chul, The Burnout Society, CA, Stanford University Press, 2015, 8.
4. Ibid., 19.
5. Ibid., 49.
6. Nagoski, Emily 'et al.', Burnout - The Secret to unlocking the stress cycle, New York, Penguin Random House LLC, 2019, xiii.
7. Ibid., xi-xii.
8. Fruedenberger, Herbert, "Staff Burn-out syndrome, 1975, and Burnout, quoted by Nagoski and Nagoski
9. Ibid. Web.
10. Maslach, Christina. Web.
11. Maslach, Christina and Jackson, Susan. 1981. Web.
12. DuBois, Allison and Mistretta, Molly, "Overcoming Burnout and Compassion Fatigue in Schools", Web.
13. Han, Byung-Chul, The Burnout Society, CA, Stanford University Press, 2015, 44.
14. Beavis, Wes, Avoiding Ministry Burnout, from his research
15. Godin, Seth, The Practice, NY, Penguin Random House, 2020, 61.
16. Hart, Archibald, The Hidden Link Between Adrenaline and Stress, Thomas Nelson, 1995. Throughout.
17. McKeown, Greg, Effortless, NY, Penguin Random House LLC, 2021, 7.
18. Lencioni, Patrick, The Advantage, CA, Jossey-Bass, 2012,1, 3.
19. Ibid,. 5.
20. Ibid,. 9.
21. Cloud, Henry, Boundaries for Leaders, NY, Harper Designs, 2013, 62.
22. It's also referred to as "emotional contagion"
23. I got this idea from James K.A. Smith's book You are what you love
24. Godin, Seth, The Practice, NY, Penguin Random House, 2020, 6.

PART TWO

25. Brown, Brené, Atlas of the Heart, New York, Penguin Random House LLC, 2021, 258.
26. Burnett, Bill 'et al.', Designing your Life, UK, Penguin Random House, 2016, 15.
27. Soojung-Kim Pang, Alex, Shorter, NY, Hachette Book Group, 2020, 218.
28. Nagoski, Emily 'et al.', Burnout - The Secret to unlocking the stress cycle, New York, Penguin Random House LLC, 2019, xiii.
29. Please don't hear what I'm not saying here. There are terrible atrocities in our world and too many victims of these atrocities. It is inspiring when people choose to move beyond their circumstances and not be defined by them.
30. I call these identity goals and impact goals and give you a grid to develop them in this book
31. Newport, Cal, Deep Work, NY, Hachette Book Group, 2016,146.
32. Dalton-Smith, Saundra, Sacred Rest, NY, Hachette Book Group, 2017,throughout.
33. This phrase is shared repeatedly throughout his book 7 Habits of Highly Effective People

34 Dan Pink explains this throughout his book When
35 This is the refrain throughout the book Going on a Bear Hunt by Michael Rosen and Helen Oxenbury
36 This is Henri Nouwen's term and he has a book with that title
37 Brown, Brene, Braving the Wilderness, NY, Penguin Random House, 2017, 69.
38 Brooks, David, The Second Mountain, NY, Penguin Random House, 2019, xvii.
39 Chopra, Deepak MD, 'et al.', The Healing Self, NY, Penguin Random House, 2018, 34.
40 Ibid., 54.
41 Brown, Brené, Atlas of the Heart, New York, Penguin Random House LLC, 2021,
43 Steven Pressfield uses this thread of resistance throughout his book The War of Art
42 Ibid., 43.
43 This has some parallels with what some call distraction, lack of focus or spiritual warfare but is different. Steven Pressfield writes most profoundly on this topic of resistance.
44 Pressfield, Steven, The War of Art, NY, Black Irish Entertainment LLC, 2002, 8.
45 Ibid., 14.
46 Ibid., 64.
47 A conversation with the author December 8th, 2023
48 He said this during an episode of the Dadville Podcast
49 McManus, Erwin Raphael, Mind Shift, NY, Penguin Random House, 2023, 10.

PART THREE
50 Brooks, David, The Second Mountain, NY, Penguin Random House, 2019, 28.
51 Walter Brueggemann's idea
52 Richard Rohr's idea
53 St. Teresa of Avila's life and thoughts are compiled in a book with this title
54 Hyatt, Michael 'et al.' Living Forward, MI, Baker Books, 2016, 32.
55 Dictionary.com, "certainty"
56 Ibid. "clarity"
57 Miroslav Volf and a team of researchers ask this jarring question in the book Life Worth Living
58 The Six Types of Working Genius assessment was developed by Patrick Lencioni and his team at the Table Group. It's a great investment of $25 and an even better investment when you go through this with a team. I am a certified guide and love leading teams through Working Genius trainings to help them translate this into alignment and action.
59 McKeown, Greg, Effortless, NY, Penguin Random House LLC, 2021,17.
60 Henry, Todd, Herding Tigers, NY, Penguin Random House, 2018, 32.
61 Gerber, Michael, emyth.com
62 Ibid. Web.
63 Rath, Tom 'et al.', Strengths Based Leadership, NY, Gallup Press, 2008, 2-3.
64 This definition is used throughout his book The Effective Executive
65 He shares this throughout his book Trust and Inspire
66 This from from Herbert Freudenberger's thinking and original research on burn-out. Web.
67 Aristotle, Nicomachean Ethics, in The Basic Works of Aristotle, translated by Richard McKeon, New York Modern Library, 2001, 2.4.

PART FOUR
68 Mindshift Podcast, November 17, 2023
69 I highly recommend his Audible sales course "How to persuade and get paid". I found it incredibly helpful to debunking myths about sales and giving a clarifying framework.
70 Of course, there is a time for outside aid, especially in natural disasters, war and extreme circumstances.
71 Dalton-Smith, Saundra, Sacred Rest, NY, Hachette Book Group, 2017,110.
72 Burnett, Bill 'et al.', Designing your Life, UK, Penguin Random House, 2016, xv-xvi.
73 Cloud, Henry, Boundaries for Leaders, NY, Harper Designs, 2013, 86.
74 I originally heard this question in an interview with Brené Brown
75 McManus, Erwin Raphael, Mind Shift, NY, Penguin Random House, 2023, 89.
76 Brown, Brene, Braving the Wilderness, NY, Penguin Random House, 2017, 107.
77 Brown, Tim, Change By Design, NY, Harper Collins, 2019, 112.
78 Ibid., 112.
79 Burnett, Bill 'et al.', Designing your Life, UK, Penguin Random House, 2016, 98.
80 Godin, Seth, The Practice, NY, Penguin Random House, 2020,15.
81 This is Marshall Goldsmith's term and he has a great book with this title. The dude is legendary.
82 This phrase is scattered throughout Adam Grant's book Think Again
83 Newport, Cal, Deep Work, NY, Hachette Book Group, 2016, 141.
84 This is discussed frequently in his classic book 7 Habits for Highly Effective People
85 McKeown, Greg, Effortless, NY, Penguin Random House LLC, 2021,12.
86 Newport, Cal, Deep Work, NY, Hachette Book Group, 2016, 3.
87 Ibid., 6.
88 Ibid., 14.
89 McKeown, Greg, Effortless, NY, Penguin Random House LLC, 2021, 17.
90 He shares this analogy throughout his book The Practice of Adaptive Leadership
91 Nagoski, Emily 'et al.', Burnout - The Secret to unlocking the stress cycle, New York, Penguin Random House LLC, 2019, 58.
92 For a deep dive into the effects of adrenaline on leaders I recommend Archibald Hart's classic book The Hidden Link Between Adrenaline and Stress

PART FIVE
93 McKeown, Greg, Effortless, NY, Penguin Random House LLC, 2021, 51.
94 This is the foundation of his incredible book Atomic Habits
95 Soojung-Kim Pang, Alex, Shorter, NY, Hachette Book Group, 2020,14.

Made in the USA
Coppell, TX
19 January 2026